HANS WALTER WOLFF is emeritus professor of Old Testament at the University of Heidelberg and the author of many widely used studies, including *Anthropology of the Old Testament*; *Joel and Amos*; and *Obadiah and Jonah*.

MARGARET KOHL, who lives near Munich, has translated works by Ernst Käsemann, Wolfhart Pannenberg, Jürgen Moltmann, Klaus Koch, Willi Marxsen, and others, in addition to three other books by Hans Walter Wolff.

HAGGAI

HAGGAI

HANS WALTER WOLFF

HAGGAI

A Commentary

Translated by

Margaret Kohl

AUGSBURG PUBLISHING HOUSE
MINNEAPOLIS

HAGGAI
A Commentary

Library of Congress Cataloging-in-Publication Data

Wolff, Hans Walter.
  HAGGAI: a commentary.

  Bibliography: p.
  Includes indexes.
  1. Bible. O.T. Haggai—Commentaries.   I. Title.
BS1655.3.W6513   1988   224'.97077   88-10513
ISBN 0-8066-2366-7

The paper used in this publication meets the minimum requirements of American National Standard for Information Sciences—Permanence of Paper for Printed Materials, ANSI Z329.48-1984.

∞™

Manufactured in the U.S.A.   APH 10-2930

1   2   3   4   5   6   7   8   9   0   1   2   3   4   5   6   7   8   9

Dedicated to the
Honorable Board of Regents and Faculty of
SAINT OLAF COLLEGE
Northfield, Minnesota
in Gratitude for the Conferring of
the Honorary Degree of
Doctor of Divinity

Contents

9

Preface

Haggai is one of the most minor of the minor prophets, indeed one of the most despised. And yet this little book is a model of effective proclamation, in its dispute with a stubborn and dispirited people—a model in its questions and its admonitions, its encouragement and its activating promise. In a few scenes, the reader learns how the listeners to its message are led from the soreness of failure into a "hope of glory."

Like its predecessors, this part of the exposition of the Book of the Twelve Prophets attempts to pursue all the important problems raised by contemporary research. In doing so I have to acknowledge a debt to the brothers and fathers from whom I have gratefully learned. After 35 years of work on this series of biblical commentaries, both as author and as one of its editors, I should also like to thank the Neukirchener Verlag for the enterprising spirit with which—under its editorial manager, Johannes Meyer-Stoll, and the director of the Neukirchener Erziehungsverein, Pastor Kirchhoff—it set out on this extensive venture in the first difficult years after the Second World War. Year after year, during Holy Week, the publishers have enabled all the authors concerned to meet for valuable days of scholarly exchange; and every volume has been knowledgeably and skillfully prepared for press by the publishing staff. The volumes are appearing more slowly than was originally planned. But the unexpectedly large number of subscribers—a number that is still growing, in spite of increased costs—should surely encourage both publishers and authors to press on unflaggingly towards the completion of the whole series.

This slender volume is dedicated to St. Olaf College, Minnesota, in gratitude for my kind reception into the college's community of teaching and research.

HANS WALTER WOLFF

Translator's Preface

The lucidity of Professor Wolff's commentary on the book of Haggai would seem to make an extensive translator's preface superfluous. But a few explanatory remarks about points of detail may be of service to the reader.

Professor Wolff has translated his text directly from the Hebrew, and the English version adheres to the German as closely as possible, precision taking precedence over stylistic elegance. Where no modification was required for a correct rendering of the German text, however, the Revised Standard Version of the Bible has been retained as basis for the English text. The names of persons and places also follow the spelling of this version. Professor Wolff left the Hebrew, Greek, and Latin readings untranslated in his textual commentary, but here English translations have been supplied, the original readings being retained in addition.

A list of abbreviations, including manuscript sigla, will allow the reader to pursue bibliographical references.

The use of brackets in the biblical text may need a word of explanation. Words enclosed in round brackets, i.e. ( ), complete the sense but are not explicitly included in the Hebrew text. Words within square brackets, i.e. [ ], are considered by the author to be interpolations. Words within angle brackets, i.e. 〉 〈 are textual emendations discussed in the notes.

An asterisk appended to verse references in the text (e.g., 2:15-19*) represents what the author considers, on the basis of textual criticism, to be the text in its original form, reasons being given in the discussion.

The *Chronicler* (with capital letter) refers to the tradition of Ezra, Nehemiah, and the books of Chronicles. The *chronicler,* in our present context, is the final editor of the book of Haggai (see the discussion in the commentary).

A very few minor changes and corrections to the German text have been made in consultation with Professor Wolff. To him my thanks are once again due for much kindness, and for his patient help and cooperation. I am also grateful to the publishers for their consideration throughout, and especially to Dr. Marshall Johnson, editor of academic books, for his scrupulously careful editing.

MARGARET KOHL

13

Introduction

1. Haggai's Time

Haggai's time is a short time, and more accurately fixed than that of any other prophet. His sayings are dated, and belong within three and a half months during the second half of the year 520 B.C.: the 1st day of the 6th month of the 2nd year of King Darius (= August 29, 520: see 1:1); the 24th day of the 6th month of the same year (= September 21: see 1:15a); the 21st day of the 7th month (= October 17: see 1:15b—2:1); and the 24th day of the 9th month, 520 (= December 18, 520: see 2:10a, 18b, 20).

It is the end of the exilic period. The dark shadows of the catastrophe of 587 are still hanging heavy over Jerusalem. The temple, which had burned to the ground, is still a heap of rubble, the haunt of jackals (Hag. 1:4, 9; Lam. 5:18). It is true that in the first year of his reign (538) Cyrus had already ordered that the Jerusalem sanctuary be rebuilt (Ezra 6:3). But the work which Sheshbazzar, as "governor," had then put in hand had done hardly anything to change the somber picture, even after 18 years (Ezra 5:14-16).

Stronger contingents of people returning from Babylonian exile were needed before the rebuilding which Cyrus had made possible could be carried out. These larger groups of homecomers probably arrived during the second half of the reign of Cyrus's son Cambyses, no doubt in connection with his Egyptian campaigns (525—522); or they may have come during the transition to Darius's rule in 522—521. They were led by Zerubbabel, who had been appointed governor of Judah (Hag. 1:1, 12, 14; 2:2, 4, 21, 23; cf. Ezra 2:2; also p. 38 below). This offered prophets like Haggai a new chance to spur the people on. Hope for the rebuilding of the temple flickered up once more.

People were also exercised in mind because of news from the outposts of the Persian empire. From 522 to 521 Darius I Hystaspes (see pp. 36 and 74-76 below) had to fight against numerous rebels, so that it was more than a year before he could establish his rule over a huge empire, stretching from the Nile almost to the Indus (see p. 75 below). It was about this time that Haggai appeared on the scene. On the one hand, therefore, Jerusalem enjoyed peace, since the struggles of the various rivals were mainly fought out further east. On the other hand, there were groups who were sensitive to any unusual action with a public impact. This meant that the tension arising between the Persian province of Judah and the neighboring province of Samaria about participation in the building of the temple (Ezra 4: 1-5; Hag. 2:14 and p. 92 below) was bound to lead at the very least to political controls in Jerusalem. And, according to Ezra 5:3-10, these were in fact enforced with the visitation of Tattenai, the satrap of Abarnahara, who came to Jerusalem from Damascus during the building of the temple (see p. 39 below).

So when Haggai urged that the building of the temple should be put in hand, his exhortations sent out ripples into the very heart of the Persian empire (Ezra 5:11—6:13). With the Persian king's help, the second temple was completed in the space of only 4½ years, whereas 7½ years had been needed to build Solomon's temple (cf. Hag. 1:1, 15a,b—2:1; Ezra 6:15 with 1 Kings 6:1, 37f.). The prophetic word of only a few months had far-reaching results. The scattered people found its old rallying point once more—one that was now to serve it for another 500 years. The brief era of prophetic efficacy brought about the turn of an age.

2. Haggai the Man

There is only one person in the Old Testament called Haggai—the prophet who came on to the scene in the second half of the year 520 B.C. and whose proclamation has been passed down to us as the tenth in the Book of the Twelve Prophets. In this book his name is mentioned nine times (1:1, 3, 12, 13; 2:1, 10, 13, 14, 20). He is also mentioned in Ezra 5:1; 6:14, in conjunction with Zechariah. For chronological reasons (cf. Hag. 1:1 with Zech. 1:1) Haggai is mentioned first, just as he precedes Zechariah in the Book of the Twelve Prophets.

Haggai was a favorite name in the Old Testament world. We have evidence of this from Hebrew seals, Aramaic sources, and also Akkadian and Egyptian parallels (see p. 37 below). The reason why the name was so widespread was its meaning: to be born on a feast day (חג) counted as a good omen. The name echoes the rejoicing over the child's birth: "My feast-day's joy!" (see p. 37 below).

Our Old Testament Haggai is called "the prophet" five times by his chronicler (1:1, 3, 12; 2:1, 10). He is also twice given the same title in the Aramaic chronicle in the book of Ezra (5:1; 6:14). The first transmitter of Haggai's sayings once emphasizes specially that he was "the messenger of Yahweh" (1:13; see pp. 32f. below), a title that is otherwise applied to a prophet only in Isa. 44:26 and 2 Chron. 36:15f. This in itself would be reason enough to keep us from seeing him as "cultic prophet," even though his zeal for the rebuilding of the Jerusalem temple has led to his being viewed in that light. But what speaks against this conclusion is not only his frequent use of the classic messenger-speech formula (1:2, 5, 7, 8; 2:6, 7, 9a, 11) and the divine-oracle formula ("saying of Yahweh," 1:9, 13; 2:8, 9, 14, 17 and three times in 2:4 and 2:23 respectively; see excursus on p. 100 below); he also confronts priestly questions almost as if they are something he finds alien (2:11-13). On the other hand, he addresses the high priest with as much self-assurance as he does the governor (1:1, 12, 14; 2:2, 4). His exertions on behalf of the building of the temple are sustained by an ardent future expectation (2:6-9, 21f., 23). Haggai therefore impressed the postexilic community as being a prophet with extraordinary authority. And his confidence, firing his critical energy, led to success (Hag. 1:12-14; Ezra 5:1f.; 6:14).

It is more difficult to answer the question whether Haggai belonged to the original group of Judaeans who had never been deported, or whether he was one of the *gola,* or exiles, who returned home with Zerubbabel and Joshua. He is not mentioned in the list of homecomers in Ezra 2/Nehemiah 7, and he does not utter a single word suggesting any recollection of the exile (as Zechariah does, e.g., 1:14ff.; 2:6ff.; 6:15). On the other hand, he does show a lively interest in farming problems in his home country (1:6, 10f.; 2:16, 19). All this could suggest that he belonged to the country people who had remained at home, and that it was as such that he addressed Zerubbabel and Joshua, the governor and the high priest, who were the leaders of the people who had returned from exile.

We are not told directly how old Haggai was, any more than we are directly told about the duration of his activity. A good 3½ months of "ministry" are securely dated (see p. 9 above). W. Rudolph deduces from 1:2f. that the opinion of the people recorded in v. 2 was a reaction to an earlier proclamation on Haggai's part. But this deduction becomes uncertain once we assume that the redactional dating is accurate and complete, and that it has been reworked by the Haggai chronicler out of sketches of scenes in which Haggai played the lead (see p. 33 below). Nor can we conclude with certainty from 2:3 that Haggai himself was one of the people who in 520 could still remember the beauty of the temple destroyed in 587— which would make him more than 70 years old. It is certainly curious that the transmission of Haggai's sayings, which initiated and accompanied the building of the temple, should break off after only 3½ months. Did Haggai die soon after December 18, 520?

3. The Book of Haggai

The final form of the book of Haggai as we have it presents four accounts of the confronting event of God's word (*Wortereignis*) (1:1-15a; 1:15b—2:9; 2:10-19; 2:20-23). These are given five different dates (1:1; 1:15a; 1:15b—2:1; 2:10; 2:20) and very probably go back to prophetic admonitions or exhortations delivered by Haggai on five different occasions (1:1-14; 1:15a + 2:15-19*; 1:15b—2:9*; 2:10-14; 2:20-23); see pp. 59f. below.

Three "growth rings" can be detected in the transmission of these accounts. The center is *the prophetic proclamation* delivered on Haggai's five appearances (1:4-11; 2:15-19*; 2:3-9*; 2:14; 2:21b-23*). This body of prophetic sayings does not derive from the prophet in the literary sense; the autobiographical "I" never appears. We are probably indebted for the sayings to a pupil or disciple (cf. Isa. 8:16; Jeremiah 36), who in *sketches of scenes* in which Haggai appeared (see pp. 33, 72 and frequently) preserved not merely the prophetic words recorded, but also the history of their effect (1:12b-13) or the history that preceded them (2:11-13), as well as the opposition of Haggai's listeners (1:2).

The introductions, announcing the confronting event of the word, constitute the outer ring (1:1-3; 1:15a; 1:15b—2:2; 2:10; 2:20-21a). These regularly append to the actual text of the scene-sketch the date of the utterance (which is why we call this final editor *the Haggai chronicler*). These introductions also generally add a pointer to the confronting event of Yahweh's word, and a mention of Haggai as the medium or receiver (see p. 37 below) of that word. Finally the addressees of the prophetic word are named. It was probably also the chronicler who took over the people's protest in 1:2b; he was no doubt able to take this from the older beginning of the scene-sketch before 1:4ff. This is also suggested by the messenger formula in 1:2a, which does not fit v. 2b, but is in line with the language of the scene-sketches (see p. 32 below). The chronicler needs 1:2 as an introduction to the description of the situation. Afterwards, in v. 3, he again picks up from v. 1 the —for him typical—formula for the confronting event of God's word, as well as the specific reference to "the prophet" Haggai as mediator, again in accordance with the wording of v. 1. The Haggai chronicler probably also separated 2:15-19* from 1:15a, placing it after 2:10-14 (see p. 61 below). Moreover, the chronicler has occasionally intervened in, and supplemented, the scene-sketches which he has taken over. Examples of such intervention are the address to the high priest Joshua in 2:4 (see p. 73 below), the "But now" at the beginning of 2:15 (see p. 42 below) and the dating given in 2:18b (see p. 61f. below). (For a discussion of the two phases of the Haggai chronicle, see pp. 35f. and 98-99 below.)

Other additions must be seen as later *interpolations* (2:5aα, 17; the two last words in 2:18 and the first four words in 2:19aβ, as well as the more considerable expansions of the Septuagint at the end of verses 2:9, 14, 21, 22bα). It must be pointed out in general that, while a distinction can be made in principle between the scene-sketches and the Haggai chronicle, the assignment of individual later additions to one or the other is bound to remain a more uncertain matter.

However, the distinction between the scene-sketches, as the literary core, and the Haggai chronicle, as the determining final redaction, is of the first importance for the book's genesis. The reasons will be given in the course of the commentary. Here I should like merely to gather together the cogent evidence, together with some probable conclusions, insofar as these are of value for the discussion.

The language of the Haggai chronicler can be unmistakably distinguished from that of the scene-sketches. This is made particularly clear in the doublet 1:12b-

13 and 1:12a, 14. In the scene-sketch the addressee of Yahweh's word is—twice—simply "the people" (12b, 13a). The chronicler, on the other hand, names the governor, the high priest, and "all the remnant of the people" (12a, 14a; cf. 1:1 with 2:2). The scene-sketch calls Haggai "Yahweh's messenger" (13a), which is unusual; the chronicler calls him "the prophet" (12a, as almost always in the chronicler's introductions announcing the event of Yahweh's word: 1:1, 3; 2:1, 10). The effect of the prophetic word is accordingly described differently (cf. 12a, 14 with 12b, 13; see pp. 49-50 below).

In the rest of the book the Haggai chronicler regularly talks about the confronting event of God's word ("The word of Yahweh came by . . .": 1:1, 3; 2:1, 10, 20), whereas the scene-sketches 8 times uses the messenger formula, "thus has Yahweh said," and 12 times the divine-oracle formula, "saying of Yahweh (Sebaoth)," even when it does not fit the present context (as in 1:2) or seems superfluous, because it is parallel to the formula for the confronting event of God's word (cf. 2:10b with 2:11a). It is also noticeable that in 2:10-14 the chronicler calls Haggai "the prophet" (2:10), which is his regular practice (except for 2:20; see p. 10 above and pp. 98f. below), whereas the prophet's pupil or disciple talks simply about "Haggai" (2:13, 14).

The point that is particularly noteworthy for a consideration of the book's genesis is that the scene-sketches name as addressee "the people" (1:2, 12b, 13a) or "the whole people of the land" (2:4), whereas the chronicler stresses, and names first, Zerubbabel, the governor of Judah, and the high priest, Joshua (1:1), and after that "all the remnant of the people" (1:12a, 14; 2:2; on 2:4 see p. 73 below). In 2:21 the Haggai chronicler mentions only "Zerubbabel, governor of Judah" as addressee, whereas the saying itself in the scene-sketch (v. 23) addresses Zerubbabel (without the Persian governor-title) as Yahweh's servant. In the scene-sketch, the title "governor of Judah" is already missing in 2:4, although it is carefully noted in the chronicler's introduction in 2:2; cf. 1:12a and p. 51 below. In view of these observations, the distinction between the scene-sketches and the Haggai chronicle must surely be deemed indispensable, even if a few problems still remain.

But what process led from the collection of the scene-sketches to the Haggai chronicle, with its accounts of the event of God's word? How, that is to say, did our present book of Haggai come into being? The end of the scene-sketches throws light on this, and it is here that we must seek for the answer. It is only Haggai's last saying to Zerubbabel that fully brings out the great importance of the governor of Judah as Yahweh's servant. It would be impermissible to separate this special form of address—and above all the description of Zerubbabel as "signet ring"—from the general theme of the book of Haggai. But if this is conceded, 2:23 must mean that it is Zerubbabel who is going to complete and seal the building of the temple (cf. Zech. 4:9). In the earlier groups of sayings, Zerubbabel is mentioned once at most (2:4; on the problem here see pp. 72f. below). Neither in 1:4-11 nor in 2:15-19 nor in 2:3-9 does he play an essential part in what Haggai says. As a rule the frequent second person plural seems to be addressed to the people as a whole. It was only during the weeks between the 1st day of the 6th month (= August 29) and the 24th day of the 9th month (= December 18) that the great importance of the governor became clear. Haggai's very first collection of sayings in 1:4-11 is therefore pinpointed and docketed for Zerubbabel and Joshua in 1:1; the reaction of the people to whom Haggai's message was addressed first of all is communicated to the governor as impeachment, as it were (1:1-2). But what is now especially noticeable is the way in which the reaction of the people is described in 1:12-14. Whereas the prophet's disciple had talked only about the godly fear of "the people" (1:12b), in vv. 12a and 14 the Haggai chronicler talks about the rousing of Zerubbabel and Joshua and "all the remnant of the people." But this in fact means that it was the governor of Judah (who had recently returned home) and the high priest and all those who had returned from exile with them who followed Haggai's call—not "the people" as a whole and per se. This closer definition is repeated in 2:2 and 4 (see pp. 72f. below).

Is this not intended to reflect the decision of the fourth scene in 2:14, which excluded the "unclean" Samaritans from joining in work on the temple? According to Ezra 4:1-5 it was also Zerubbabel who had to implement this decision. This would mean that it is the clarifications in the two scenes of the 24th day of the 9th month (= December 18)—the decision about "the unclean" and the consoling encouragement to Zerubbabel—which provided the motivation for the revisions of the Haggai chronicle. An essential point here was the assignment of 2:15-19 to 2:10-14, so that the turn to salvation did not already come about on the 24th day of the 6th month (= September 21), but only followed once Samaritan help had been rejected, on the 24th day of the 9th month (= December 18); see p. 62 below.

But what bearing does this have on the genesis of the book of Haggai? According to the testimony of the scene-sketches, Haggai, step by step, led all the people available to rebuild the temple. But the Haggai chronicle, which we have before us in the final version of the book, shows that in fact the essential measures were initiated by the governor, Zerubbabel, and by his group of returning exiles. And Haggai himself was brought to make this decision, according to his last two appearances on the scene.

4. Haggai's Language

If Haggai made an essential contribution to the assumption of work on the second temple—in spite of very great difficulties—this was due not least to the impressive character of his language.

Above all, he and his disciples were convinced that he was an authorized *messenger of Yahweh* (see the comment on 1:13a below). Thus in the 24 verses which in all probability reproduce his prophetic sayings, there are no fewer than 23 word forms (verbs, nouns, and pronominal forms) representing the "I" of Yahweh himself. The messenger formula (used 8 times) and the divine-oracle formula (12 times) are correspondingly frequent. Haggai 2:23 shows in an exemplary and impressive way how the thrice-used divine-oracle formula stresses Yahweh's "I" word for word; see the excursus on the oracle formula, p. 100 below.

But a no less prominent feature of Haggai's language is the clear predominance of sentences of direct *address* to his listeners. In the 24 verses which reproduce his own words, there are 27 word forms (pronouns, suffixes, and affixes) belonging to the second person plural, and 5 belonging to the second person singular. The lively dialog character of his style is illustrated by the unusually large number of imperatives—10 in all (1:5, 7; 2:15, 18a; three each in 1:8a and 2:4a, cj.)—and by no less than 8 questions (1:4, 9; 2:16a cj.; 2:19a [two: see p. 59 below] and three in 2:3). This debating style is almost stormily emphatic. It does not relax its hold on its listeners, as Haggai sets them before his God.

It is therefore not surprising that, among the linguistic genres used, *the admonition* should play a prominent part. It leads mainly to insight into guilt (1:5b, 7b) and to a recognition of the changeover from the time of trouble to the time of blessing (2:15a, 18a). Even when the admonition is also *an exhortation* to specific action (1:8a; 2:4) it is backed up, not by threats of judgment, as one might perhaps expect, but always by assurances of salvation (1:8b; 2:4b, 6-9; 2:19). And it is in line with this that the book should close with an unconditional promise (2:23).

When the guiding admonitions bring about insight into guilt, this involves *a transformation of earlier genres*. The "futility" curses become sayings recording curses that have been fulfilled (1:6, 9a; see p. 44 below). The justificatory judgment speeches of the classical prophets become an argumentative account tracing back present troubles (1:9a) to continued guilt (1:9b-10) and to the fulfillment of an earlier judgment speech (1:11). Stringent argumentation ("why?"— "because"—"therefore," 1:9b-10) picks up the justificatory "didactic interpretation of history" from Deuteronomistic texts (cf. 1 Kings 9:7-9 and p. 47 below). Everything that is important is gathered together under the admonition urging the people to recognize their guilt.

Little stylistic devices accentuate *the urgency* of the speech. The alliteration חֹרֶב—חָרֵב (1:4, 9, 11) intensifies the connection between the devastated temple and the parched land. The antithesis "your house" — "Yahweh's house" (1:4, 9b) unmistakably interlocks guilt and trouble. A didactic statement (2:8) gives extra force to the promises (2:7, 9a). Assurances of support (1:13b; 2:4b, 5aβ,b) accompany the main admonitions. A legal judgment (2:14) transposes comparable sayings from the priestly torah (2:11-13) into a judgment with severe consequences. A unique threat of downfall addressed to all the armed forces of the nations (2:21b-22) merely indicates the reverse side of the promise to the temple community (cf. 2:6f., 23).

All in all, the force and variety of Haggai's language and speech forms— in a mere five discourses—helped to raise a building of new beauty out of the rubble, a building that was to become the center of Judaism for the next 500 years. As a model of didactic language, Haggai's sayings can offer impulses for all kinds of building in the community of God's people.

5. Haggai's Message

Haggai is impelled by a single question: how can the devastated temple in Jerusalem be rebuilt? His success (Ezra 6:14f.) reflects an unusual capacity for motivating other people through his own energy.

On his first appearance on the stage, we become aware that Haggai is driven by a double impulse: on the one hand, by a perception of guilt, which traces back a drought from which the people are suffering to neglect of work on the temple (1:4-6, 9-11); on the other, by the promise assuring Yahweh's glorious presence to the people who put their hands to the work (1:8).

The second scene brings out the significance of the promise as incentive to the work: the day when building is begun means the turn from curse to blessing (2:15f., 18a, 19; see pp. 66f. below). It is not only the completion of the building on which Yahweh's blessing is conferred; the very first turn to obedience is already blessed.

The third scene counters reluctance to work with two further incentives: the unconditional, repeated promise of divine support (2:4b, 5aβ,b) and a threefold expansion of the promise. This expansion lends a universal dimension to the material help promised (2:6f.), so that the beauty of even Solomon's temple will be actually surpassed (2:8-9a); and Yahweh will then confer complete salvation from the sanctuary (2:9b).

In the fourth scene the expansion of the promise is followed by a restriction of the people who are to be allowed to take part in the work (2:14). The harsh judgment "impurity is infectious" counters the expectations of false helpers.

The fifth scene once again shows first of all the universal horizon of Haggai's prophecy. The saying about the foreign nations relieves Zerubbabel of all fear of the armed powers (2:21-22; see pp. 107-108 below). In addition Zerubbabel, as Yahweh's servant and the leader of the community of returning exiles, is appointed authorized guarantor of the temple's completion (2:23; cf. Zech. 4:9). The fullness of the promises which have contributed essentially to the building of the temple therefore at the end take a personified form. With Zerubbabel the God of Israel puts his seal to the promise of his presence, his blessing and peace (1:8b; 2:9b, 19b).

Haggai's efficacious message was fulfilled after five years, as far as the temple was concerned (Ezra 6:14f.). According to the New Testament, another, instead of Zerubbabel, was after more than 500 years to become the representative of God's blessing and peace.

Haggai belongs among the harbingers of this later one, since he urges that what is required in the present should be performed in the perspective of what is final and ultimate. He exhorts his people to perceive anew the glory of God's house, rising above the rubble of the curse of judgment, and to see revolutionary events in the world of the nations in relation to the old and new people of God, and to its Messiah.

6. Literature

For literature on the minor prophets up to 1976 see H. W. Wolff, *Obadiah and Jonah: A Commentary* (1986) 23-27.

1. *Commentaries on Haggai:* H. Ewald, *Die Propheten des Alten Bundes* III (1841, 1868[2]). C. F. Keil, *Biblischer Commentar über die zwölf kleinen Propheten*, BC III/4 (1866, 1888[3]). C. von Orelli, *Die zwölf kleinen Propheten*, KK V/2 (1888, 1908[3]). J. Wellhausen, *Die kleinen Propheten übersetzt und erklärt* (1892, 1898[3] = 1963[4]). T. André, *Le prophète Aggée* (1895). G. A. Smith, *The Book of the Twelve Prophets*, Expositor's Bible (1896, 1928[2]). W. Nowack, *Die Kleinen Propheten*, HAT III/4 (1897, 1922[3]). K. Marti, *Das Dodekapropheton*, KHC (1904). A. van Hoonacker, *Les douze petits prophètes*, ÉtB (1908). B. Duhm, "Anmerkungen zu den zwölf Propheten," *ZAW* 31 (1911), 1-43, 81-110, 161-204. H.G. Mitchell, *Haggai and Zechariah*, ICC (1912, 1961[2]). M. Haller, *Das Judentum*, Die Schriften des Alten Testaments II/3 (1914, 1925[2]). O. Procksch, *Die kleinen prophetischen Schriften*, EzAT II (1916), 1929[2]). E. Sellin, *Das Zwölfprophetenbuch*, KAT XII/2 (1922, 1930[2,3]). P.F. Bloomhardt, "The Poems of Haggai," *HUCA* 5 (1928) 153-195. J. Ridderbos, *De kleine Profeten* III (Haggai—Malachi), KVHS (1930, 1952[2]). H. Junker, *Die zwölf kleinen Propheten* II, HSAT(K), VIII/3/II (1938). F. Horst (T. H. Robinson, F. Horst), *Die zwölf kleinen Propheten*, HAT I/14 (1938, 1964[3]). H. Frey *Das Buch der Kirche in der Weltwende: Die kleinen nachexilischen Propheten*, Botschaft des Alten Testaments 24 (1941, 1963[5]). F. Nötscher, *Zwölfprophetenbuch*, Echter-Bibel (1948, 1957[2]). J. A. Bewer, *The Book of the Twelve Prophets*, HAB (1949). J. Coppens, *Les douze petits prophètes* (1950). K. Elliger, *Das Buch der zwölf kleinen Propheten* II, ATD 25/II (1950, 1975[7]). M. Schumpp, *Das Buch der zwölf Propheten*, HBK X/2 (1950). D. Deden, *De kleine Profeten (Nahum-Malachias)*, De Boeken van het Oude Testament XII/7-12 (1956). K. F. T. Laetsch, *The Minor Prophets*, Bible Commentary St. Louis, Mo. (1956). D. W. Thomas, *The Book of Haggai*, IB VI (1956), 1035-1050. K. D. Bucholtz, *Haggai — Sacharja —Maleachi*, Stuttgarter Bibelhefte (1960). A. Gelin, *Aggée — Zacharie — Malachie*, Bibel de Jérusalem: Études annexes (1960, 1973[2]). P. R. Ackroyd, *Haggai — Zechariah*, PCB (1962) 643-651. J. H. Gailey Jr., *Micah to Malachi*, LBC 15 (1962). D. R. Jones, *Haggai, Zechariah and Malachi*, TBC (1962). A. M. Bonnardière, *Les douze petits prophètes*, Bibliothèque augustinienne (1963). A. Deissler, *Les petits prophètes*, SB (PC) VIII (1964) 473-499. J. L. Koole, *Haggai*, Commentar op het Oude Testament (1967). T. Chary, *Aggée—Zacharie—Malachie*, SBi (1969). D. J. Wiseman, *Haggai*, New Bible Commentary (1970[3]) 781-785. J. G. Baldwin, *Haggai, Zechariah, Malachi*, TOTC (1972). G. Fohrer, *Die Propheten des ausgehenden 6. und des 5. Jh.*, Die Propheten des Alten Testaments 5 (1976) 37-49. W. Rudolph, *Haggai — Sacharja 1-8 — Sacharja 9-14 — Maleachi*, KAT XIII/4 (1976) 19-58. R. A. Mason, *The Books of Haggai, Zechariah and Malachi*, CBC (1977). F. J. Stendebach,

Prophetie und Tempel: Haggai — Sacharja — Maleachi — Joel, Stuttgarter Kleiner Kommentar (1977). S. Amsler (S. Amsler, A. Lacocque, R. Vuilleumier), *Aggée (— Zacharie — Malachie),* CAT XIc (1981) 11-42. A. S. van der Woude, *Haggai, Maleachi,* De Prediking van het Oude Testament (1982) 7-76. D. L. Petersen, *Haggai and Zechariah,* OTL (1984).

2. *General Studies on Haggai:* H. Bardtke, "Haggai," *EKL* II (1958) 5f. R. Bach, "Haggai, Haggaibuch," *RGG*³ III (1959) 24-26. W. Neil, "Haggai," *IDB* 2 (1962) 509-511. J. Lindblom, *Prophecy in Ancient Israel* (1963). M. L. Henry, "Haggai," *BHH* II (1964) 624f. I. H. Eybers, "Haggai: The Mouthpiece of the Lord," *Theologia Evangelica* 1 (1968) 62-71. K. Koch, *The Prophets II: Babylonian and Persian Periods,* trans. M. Kohl (1983), 159-175. H. W. Wolff, "Haggai/Haggaibuch," *TRE* 14 (1985) 355-360.

3. *Textual Criticism:* K. Budde, "Zum Text der drei letzten kleinen Propheten," *ZAW* 26 (1906) 1-28 (7-17). A. B. Ehrlich, *Randglossen zur hebräischen Bibel* V (1912; reprint 1968) 319-324.

4. *Literary Problems and Redaction History:* W. Böhme, "Zu Maleachi und Haggai," *ZAW* 7 (1887) 210-217 (215f.). E. Sellin, *Studien zur Entstehungsgeschichte der jüdischen Gemeinde* II (1901). J. W. Rothstein, *Die Genealogie des Königs Jojachin und seiner Nachkommen (1. Chr. 3, 17-24) in geschichtlicher Beleuchtung* (1902); also *Juden und Samaritaner: Die grundlegende Scheidung von Judentum und Heidentum. Eine kritische Studie zum Buche Haggai und zur jüdischen Geschichte im ersten nachexilischen Jahrhundert,* BWAT 3 (1908). P. R. Ackroyd, "Studies in the Book of Haggai," *JJS* 2 (1951) 163-176; 3 (1952) 1-13; also "The Book of Haggai and Zechariah 1—8," *JJS* 3 (1952) 151-156; also "Some Interpretative Glosses in the Book of Haggai," *JJS* 7 (1956) 163-167; also "Two Old Testament Historical Problems of the Early Persian Period," *JNES* 17 (1958) 13-27. F. S. North, "Critical Analysis of the Book of Haggai," *ZAW* 68 (1956) 25-46. R. A. Mason, "The Purpose of the 'Editorial Framework' of the Book of Haggai," *VT* 27 (1977) 413-421. R. W. Pierce, "Literary Connectors and a Haggai/Zechariah/Malachi Corpus," *JETS* 27 (1984) 277-290.

5. *Style and Form Criticism:* J. Begrich, *Die priesterliche Tora,* BZAW 66 (1936) 63-88 = his *Gesammelte Studien zum AT,* Theologische Bücherei 21 (1964) 232-260. K. Koch, "Haggais unreines Volk," *ZAW* 79 (1967) 52-66. J. W. Whedbee, "A Question-Answer Scheme in Haggai 1: The Form and Function of Haggai 1. 9-11," *Biblical and Near Eastern Studies: Fests. W. S. LaSor,* ed. G. A. Tuttle (1978) 184-194.

6. *Tradition History:* W. A. M. Beuken, *Haggai — Sacharja 1-8: Studien*

zur Überlieferungsgeschichte der frühnachexilischen Prophetie, SSN 10 (1967).
K. M. Beyse, *Serubbabel und die Königserwartungen der Propheten Haggai und Sacharja,* AzTh I/48 (1972).

7. *Haggai the Man:* M. Noth, *Die israelitischen Personennamen im Rahmen der gemeinsemitischen Namengebung,* BWANT III/10 (1928, 1980²). F. James, "Thoughts on Haggai and Zechariah," *JBL* 53 (1934) 229-235. M. D. Coogan, *West Semitic Personal Names in the Murašû Documents,* Harvard Semitic Monographs 7 (1976). R. R. Wilson, *Prophecy and Society in Ancient Israel* (1980) 287-288. J. Blenkinsopp, *A History of Prophecy in Israel* (1983) 231-233. E. M. Myers, "The Use of tôrâ in Haggai 2.11 and the Role of the Prophet in the Restoration Community," *The Word of the Lord Shall Go Forth: Fests. D. N. Freedman,* ed. C. L. Meyers and M. O'Connor, American Schools of Oriental Research, Special Volume Series No. 1 (1983) 69-76.

8. *Haggai's Time:* A. Bentzen, "Quelques Remarques sur le mouvement messianique parmi les Juifs aux environs de l'an 520 avant J.-Chr.," *RHPhR* I/10 (1930) 493-503. O. Leuze, *Die Satrapieneinteilung in Syrien und im Zweistromlande von 520-320,* Schriften der Königsberger Gelehrten, Geisteswissenschaftliche Klasse 11/4 (1935). T. Chary, *Le prophètes et le culte à partir de l'exil* (1954). R. A. Parker and W. H. Dubberstein, *Babylonian Chronology 626 B.C.–A.D. 75* (1956). E. Janssen, *Juda in der Exilszeit,* FRLANT 69 (1956). F. I. Andersen, "Who Built the Second Temple?" *ABR* 6 (1958) 1-35. K. Baltzer, "Das Ende des Staates Juda und die Messias-Frage," *Studien zur Theologie der alttestamentlichen Überlieferungen,* ed. R. Rendtorff and K. Koch (1961) 33-43. K. Galling, "Serubbabel und der Wiederaufbau des Tempels in Jerusalem," *Verbannung und Heimkehr: Fests. W. Rudolph,* ed. A. Kuschke (1961) 67-96; also *Studien zur Geschichte Israels im persischen Zeitalter* (1964). A. Petitjean, "La mission de Zorobabel et la reconstruction du temple," *EThL* 42 (1966) 40-71. P. R. Ackroyd, *Exile and Restoration* (1968) 153-170. M. A. Dandamaev, *Persien unter den ersten Achämeniden (6. Jh. v. Chr.),* Beiträge zur Iranistik 8 (1976). T. A. Busink, *Der Tempel von Jerusalem von Salomo bis Herodes II.* (1980) chap. X: "Der Tempel Serubbabels 776-841." E. J. Bickerman, "La seconde année de Darius," *RB* 88 (1981) 23-28. S. Japhet, "Sheshbazzar and Zerubbabel," *ZAW* 94 (1982) 66-105; 95 (1983) 218-229. W. Schottroff, "Zur Sozialgeschichte Israels in der Perserzeit," *VF* 27 (1982) 46-68. R. Borger, *Die Chronologie des Darius-Denkmals am Behistun-Felsen,* NAWG (1982) 103-132. R. Borger and W. Hinz, "Die Behistun-Inschrift Darius' des Großen," *TUAT,* ed. O. Kaiser, I/4 (1984) 419-450.

9. *Haggai's Theology and Message:* L. Waterman, "The Camouflaged Purge of Three Messianic Conspirators," *JNES* 13 (1954) 73-78. R. T. Siebeneck, "The Messianism of Aggeus and Proto-Zacharias," *CBQ* 19 (1957) 312-328. H. Bardtke, *Die Erweckungsgedanke in der exilisch-nachexilischen Literatur des*

Alten Testament, BZAW 77 (1958, 1971⁴) 9-24. G. von Rad, "Die Stadt auf dem
Berge," *EvTh* 8 (1948/49) 439-447 = his *Gesammelte Studien zum AT,*
Theologische Bücherei 8 (1958) 214-224. F. Hesse, "Haggai," *Verbannung und
Heimkehr: Fests. W. Rudolph* (1961) 109-134. D. N. Freedman, "Divine Com-
mitment and Human Obligation," *Interp.* 18 (1964) 419-431. H. G. May, " 'This
People' and 'This Nation,' " *VT* 18 (1968) 190-197. K. Seybold, "Die
Königserwartung bei den Propheten Haggai und Sacharja," *Judaica* 28 (1972) 69-
78. P. D. Hanson, *The Dawn of Apocalyptic* (1975) 173-178, 240-262. R. P.
Carroll, *When Prophecy Failed* (1979) 157-168. B. S. Childs, *Introduction to the
Old Testament as Scripture* (1979) 463-471.

10. *Individual Problems and the Interpretation of Individual Passages:*
A. Fernández, "El Profeta Ageo 2,15-18 y la fundación del segundo templo,"
Bibl. 2 (1921) 206-215. F. Peter, "Zu Haggai 1,9," *ThZ* 7 (1951) 150-151. A.
Gelston, "The Foundations of the Second Temple," *VT* 16 (1966) 232-235. G.
Sauer, *Serubbabel in der Sicht Haggais und Sacharjas,* BZAW 105 (1967) 199-
207. T. N. Townsend, "Additional Comments on Haggai II 10-19," *VT* 18 (1968)
559-560. O. H. Steck, "Zu Haggai 1,2-11," *ZAW* 83 (1971) 355-379. D. L.
Petersen, "Zerubbabel and Jerusalem Temple Reconstruction," *CBQ* 36 (1974)
366-372. A. Renker, *Die Tora bei Maleachi,* Freiburger theologische Studien 112
(1979). D. J. Clark, "Problems in Haggai 2.15-19," *The Bible Translator* 34
(1983) 432-439.

11. *Literature on the Book of Haggai:* R. A. Mason, "The Prophets of the
Restoration," *Israel's Prophetic Tradition: Fests. P. R. Ackroyd,* ed. R. Coggins,
A. Phillips, M. Knibb (1962), 137-154. L. Tetzner, *Die rabbinischen Kommentare
zum Buche Haggai* (1969). C. Westermann, review of W. A. M. Beuken,
Haggai—Sacharja 1-8 (1967), *ThLZ* 94 (1969) 424-426.

12. *Aspects for Practical Theology:* A. Jepsen, *Das Zwölfprophetenbuch,*
Bibelhilfe für die Gemeinde (1937). H. W. Wolff, *Haggai,* BSt 1 (1951). G.
Krause, "Aller Heiden Trost, Haggai 2,7. Die Beweggründe für eine falsche
Übersetzung und Auslegung des Textes durch Luther," *Solange es Heute heisst:
Fests. R. Herrmann* (1957) 170-178. H. Brandenburg, *Die kleinen Propheten I-II*
(1963). J. Bright, "Aggée: Un exercice en herméneutique," *ÉTR* 44 (1969) 3-25.
R. North, *Exégèse pratique des Petits Prophètes postexiliens* (1969).

First Scene:
Time to Build the Temple?

Literature

F. Peter, "Zu Haggai 1,9," *ThZ* 7 (1951) 150-151. R. A. Parker and W. H. Dubberstein, *Babylonian Chronology 626 B.C.—A.D. 75* (1956). H. Bardtke, *Der Erweckungsgedanke in der exilisch-nachexilischen Literatur des Alten Testaments*, BZAW 77 (1958) 9-24. K. Galling, *Studien zur Geschichte Israels im persischen Zeitalter* (1964). K. Koch, "Haggais unreines Volk," *ZAW* 79 (1967) 52-66. G. Sauer, *Serubbabel in der Sicht Haggais und Sacharjas*, BZAW 105 (1967) 199-207. O. H. Steck, "Zu Haggai 1,2-11," *ZAW* 83 (1971) 355-379. D.E. Gowan, "The Use of *ya'an* in Biblical Hebrew," *VT* 21 (1971) 168-185. B. O. Long, "Two Question and Answer Schemata in the Prophets," *JBL* 90 (1971) 129-139. R. A. Mason, "The Purpose of the 'Editorial Framework' of the Book of Haggai," *VT* 27 (1977) 413-421. J. W. Whedbee, "A Question-Answer Scheme in Haggai 1: The Form and Function of Haggai 1,9-11," *Biblical and Near Eastern Studies: Fests. W. S. LaSor*, ed. G. A. Tuttle (1978) 184-194. T. A. Busink, *Der Tempel von Jerusalem von Salomo bis Herodes II* (1980), chap. X: "Der Tempel Serubabbels," 776-841. S. Japhet, "Sheshbazzar and Zerubbabel," *ZAW* 94 (1982) 66-98.

Text

1:1 In the second year of King Darius, in the sixth month, on the first day of the month, the word of Yahweh went out through the prophet Haggai[a] to Zerubbabel, the son of Shealtiel, the governor[b] of Judah, and to Joshua, the son of Jehozadak, the high priest, saying:

2 "Thus has Yahweh of hosts spoken: This people here says: [a]now the time has not yet[b] come[a] to rebuild[c] the house of Yahweh."

3 Then the word of Yahweh[a] went out through the prophet Haggai, saying:[b]

4 "Is it then a time for you yourselves[a]
   to dwell in your[b] roofed[c] houses,
      while this house is a heap of ruins?[d]"

5 Now therefore, thus has Yahweh of hosts spoken:
   "Consider how you have fared![a]

6 You have sown much
      but harvested[a] little.
   You eat,[a]
      but there is no [b]satiety.[a]
   You drink,[a]
      but there is no [b]thirst-quenching.[a]
   You clothe yourselves,[a]
      but no one[c] is warm.[a]
   And he who goes as wage earner
      works[d] into a bag with holes."

7 Thus has Yahweh of hosts spoken:
   "Consider how you have fared!

8 Go up to the hills,
      fetch[a] wood
         and build the house!
   I will take pleasure in it
      and show myself[b] in my glory,"
         Yahweh has said.

9 "[a]You have[a] hoped for much,
      and lo,[b] (it came only to) little.
   And when you brought it home,
      I blew it away.
   Why?—saying of Yahweh of hosts—
   Because of my house,
      that[c] is a heap of ruins,
   while each of you
      runs for his own house.

10 Therefore [above you][a]
      the heavens[b] withhold)their([c] dew,
         the earth withholds its produce.

11 I called the drought[a]
      upon the land and upon the hills,
   upon the grain and wine and oil
      and upon that[b] which the ground brings forth,
   upon men and cattle
      and upon all work of hands."

12 Then Zerubbabel, the son of Shaltiel,[a] and Joshua, the son of Jehozadak,
    the high priest, and all the remnant of the people, obeyed[b] the voice of
    Yahweh, their God, namely,[c] the words of the prophet Haggai, as Yahweh
    had sent him)to them(.[d]
    And the people became afraid of Yahweh.

13 Then spoke Haggai,
       the messenger of Yahweh,[a] [b]at Yahweh's charge,[b] spoke to

the people saying:
"I am with you!—saying of Yahweh."

14 But Yahweh roused the spirit of Zerubbabel, the son of Shaltiel,[a] the governor of Judah, and the spirit of Joshua, the son of Jehozadak, the high priest, and the spirit of all the remnant of the people. Then they came and took up the work on the house of Yahweh of hosts, their God.

1a Gk interpolates λέγων Εἶπον ("as spokesman. Speak…"), thus assimilating to 2:1bβ-2aα and 2:20b-21a ([נא-] אמר לאמר), in order here to distinguish clearly between the mediator of God's word (ביד, "through") and its recipient (אל, "to"); see p. 37 below. MT's briefer reading is probably the original one (contrary to the views of J. Wellhausen, B. Duhm, and K. Elliger).[1]

1b Gk (ἐκ φυλῆς Ιουδα) here as in 1:14; 2:2, 21 (on 1:12 see textual note to 1:12b below) equates פֶּחָה (the title of the Persian governor) with מִשְׁפָּחָה ("from the tribe [of Judah]"); cf. Amos 3:1f.; Mic. 2:3; Nah. 3:4 and Zech. 12:12-14; 14:17f. The fact that Zerubbabel came from the tribe of Judah (cf. 1 Chron. 2:3ff.; 3:17ff.) would seem to be more important for Gk than his official position in the Persian empire (see p. 39 below). The title פֶּחָה ought really to be translated by the equivalent Greek governor title τόπαρχος, "toparch," or ἔπαρχος, "eparch" (2 Kings 18:24; Isa. 36:9; Ezra 6:13); see O. Leuze, *Die Satrapieneinteilung …*, (1935) 36, n. 1.

2a - a MT "It is not yet the time to come, the time to build up Yahweh's house" sounds very forced (K. Marti calls it "verschroben," eccentric); it can hardly reflect the ordinary language of the people. A. S. van der Woude, 24, believes that MT is the original reading, and relates the infinitive בֹּא ("to come") in 1:2 to וַיָּבֹאוּ ("and they came") in 1:14bα. According to A. Klostermann (*Geschichte des Volkes Israel* [1896] 235) הָעֵת ("the time") in 4a could presuppose עֶת־בֹּא לֹא, "not the (appropriate) time to come." Gk (οὐχ ἥκει ὁ καιρὸς τοῦ οἰκοδομῆσαι and S, Vg, *nondum venit tempus domus Domini aedificandae* (all: "the time has not yet come to build the house of the Lord") know only a simple עֵת ("time")—the time for building, not also the time for the people "to come." So we should either, like J. Wellhausen, K. Elliger, F. Horst, KBL[3] and others, accept the vocalization עֵת בָּא (a vocalization originally proposed by F. Hitzig [1863[3]]), or—since "now" in Haggai is only found in the form עחה (1:5; 2:3, 4, 15; but cf. Ezek. 23:43; Ps. 74:6) and עֵת generally has a feminine form (A. S. van der Woude, 24)—we should assume that עֶת־בָּא עֶת־בֵּית is a dittography of the original reading עֶת־בֵּית, "the house" (BrSynt §29b; O. H. Steck *ZAW* 83 [1971] 361 n. 21).

2b For לֹא in the restrictive sense of "not yet" cf. Gen. 2:5; 29:7; Ps. 139:16; Job 22:16.

2c Literally "to be built up." For the passive infinitive *niphal* after לֹא־עֵת ("not yet time") cf. also Gen. 29:7.

3a W. Rudolph reads דְּבָרִי ("my word") instead of דבר־יהוה ("word of Yahweh"), believing that MT has misread the pronominal suffix י ("my") as an abbreviation for יהוה. The oldest texts do not lend support to this suggestion. Nor can it be justified by the pointer to the function of this conjectured reading of v. 3, according to which Yahweh himself wished through Haggai to report to his discussion partners Zerubbabel and Joshua what he had previously said to the people, in order to confute their pernicious opinion.

3b For a literary analysis of vv. 1-3 see pp. 32-33 below.

---

[1] References to authors without short titles apply to commentaries listed in the bibliography, §6, section 1, pp. 23-24 above.

4a The suffix in לכם is particularly emphasized through the separate personal pronoun, "you yourselves"; cf. Ges.-K §135d, g and Joüon, *Gr.* §146d.

4b In numerous Gk manuscripts (cf. J. Ziegler, *Duodecim prophetae: Septuaginta Gottingensis* XIII [1943, 1984³], 285, ὑμῶν ("your") is missing, as also in S, Targ and Vg. But MT's reading will be the original one, the pronominal suffix in בבתיכם ("*your* houses") being a further polemical emphasis; cf. textual note **4a** and S. Amsler, 21, n. 4.

4c BrSynt §81f.: "in your houses as covered ones"; cf. Joüon, *Gr.* §127a on the attributive accusative of state or condition (ספונים, "covered" or "roofed," without the article).

4d Cf. K. Galling, *Studien zur Geschichte* . . . (1964) 128f.

5a Jerome (*quae feceritis et passi sitis*, "what you have done and suffered") interprets דרכים, "ways," as referring to (previous) behavior and the situation that has resulted. The context here and in 1:7, and especially in 2:15, 18, is a reminder of the connection between act and destiny—what one does and what happens as a result; cf. A. S. van der Woude, 27; also p. 43 below.

6a The stressed infinitive absolute carries on the finite verb, for stylistic emphasis; cf. BrSynt §46c; Joüon, *Gr.* §123x.

6b For the unusual feminine form of the infinitive, cf. Bauer-Leander §43d. As a parallel to "satiety," שכר does not really have the (usual) meaning of being drunk (after immoderate enjoyment). In this context what is clearly meant is not having enough to drink.

6c לו as a preposition with an indefinite pronoun points to "someone or other"; cf. Joüon, *Gr.* §152f.

6d Two manuscripts and T. André (1895) change the participle into an imperfect, but this seems unnecessary.

8a The perfect clause והבאתם, "and fetch," belongs syntactically to the series of imperatives (עלו ... ובנו, "go up ... and build") but, as indication of purpose, belongs more closely to the first imperative than to the second (ובנו, "and build"). Gk translates freely κόψατε, "cut down," but this does not necessarily mean that it read וּבְרֵא חָם (III ברא *pi'el*, "clear," cf. Josh. 17:18), the view taken by K. Budde (1906) and now by A. S. van der Woude. Vg *portate*, "bring," supports MT.

8b The *Qere* has the cohortative ואכבדה. On the cohortative following the imperative cf. BrSynt §135c, The *Ketib* text, with imperfect meaning, is probably the older reading. On the permissive meaning of the *niphal* cohortative, cf. P. R. Ackroyd, *Exile* (1968) 160, n. 32. See p. 46 below. It is not necessary to supply בו as does W. Rudolph, together with S.

9a-a The tense of the infinitive absolute, like its logical subject, is determined by the following context; cf. Joüon, *Gr.* §§123u-w; 155i.

9b Gk καὶ ἐγένετο, "and it came to pass," S,Targ, Vg *factum est*, "it was so," do not necessarily presuppose וְהָיָה but can also derive from MT, especially since Vg's *ecce*, "behold," confirms MT's והנה.

9c הוא (third pers. masc. pronoun) puts the relative clause in emphatic relation to its main word ביתי, "my house" (BrSynt §152a) and in opposition to the following אתם, "you," in correspondence to the contrasting parallels ביתי—ביתו, "my house—his house."

10a Gk has no phrase corresponding to עליכם ("because of you") and it has therefore—ever since J. Wellhausen—often been viewed as a dittography of על־כן ("therefore") and excised. S also confirms the shorter text, in that על־כן is missing. To have על־כן and עליכם side by side provides an improbable doubling of the reason. This is not avoided by viewing the preposition in עליכם in a local sense ("over you"), for the following threats do not correspond (cf. 10b). The addition of עליכם could go back to a certain formal compulsion through the Deuteronomistic, didactic view of salvation history; cf. Deut. 29:26; 1 Kings 9:9 and p. 47 below.

10b   The evidence for השמים ("the heavens") is weak, and the article is not absolutely required, even in the light of Zech. 8:12; Hag. 2:6, 21. The absence of the article in a series (cf. 2:12), being somewhat rare, speaks in favor of MT.

10c   Instead of MT's מִטָּל ("without dew") we should probably read טַלָּם "their dew" (KBL³ 359, 453). The shifting of the מ is supported not only by Zech. 8:12 but also by the grammatical link with כלאו ("withhold") and the parallel to v. 10b. Targ (מטרא) presupposes מָטָר ("rain"), which is the reading F. Horst assumes for MT also. Gk ἀπὸ δρόσου ("without dew") supports MT. Cf. also A. S. van der Woude, 33f.

11a   Gk ῥομφαίαν, "sword," is based on a mistaken vocalization, חֶרֶב.

11b   Numerous manuscripts presuppose וְעַל־כָּל, as premature climax of the long series, and in anticipation of the ועל כל in bβ. Thus some Gk manuscripts read ἐπὶ πάντα, "whatever"; similarly Vg *quaecumque*, Targ כל. The older Gk manuscripts support MT.

12a   In distinction from 1:1; 2:23, a shortened form of the name is used here, as in 1:14 and 2:2: M. Noth (*Die israelitischen Personennamen*, [1928] 63 n. 7) believes that this is the correct form and that שאלתיאל (Shealtiel) in 1:1; 2:23 is popular etymology. Gk adds after the name ἐκ φυλῆς Ιουδα "from the tribe of Judah"; cf. here textual note to 1:1b.

12b   The singular verb form can precede a plural subject; cf. Gen. 24:61; 31:14; Num. 12:1; Amos 8:13f., also Ges. K §146f.; Joüon, *Gr.* §150q.

12c   The expansion in 12aβ introduced with ו has an explanatory function (expressed here through the translation "namely"); cf. Ges. K §154, n. 1b on *wāw explicativum:* also KBL³, 248a No. 5.

12d   Gk πρὸς αὐτούς, Vg *ad ipsos* (both "to them") presuppose אֲלֵיהֶם; MT אֱלֹהֵיהֶם ("their God") is evidently a misreading, probably influenced by the preceding יהוה אלהיהם ("Yahweh, their God") in 12aα.

13a-a   Targ (נביא דיהי) assimilates to 1:1, 3, 12; 2:1, 10.

13b-b   במלאכות יהוה, "at Yahweh's charge," is generally left untranslated in Gk. Only a few manuscripts understand the word, which is unique in the Old Testament (ἐν ἀποστολῇ κυρίου, "in the mission [or 'at the commission'] of the Lord," Gᴸ and others); other manuscripts personalize it: ἐν ἀγγέλοις κυρίου, "through the messengers of the Lord" (Gᴮ and others); so also Vg, *de nuntiis Domini*, "from the messengers of Yahweh" (cf. J. Ziegler, *Duodecim prophetae: Septuaginta Gottingensis* XIII [1943, 1984³]).

14a   See textual note **1:12b** above.

Form

Like the book of Zechariah, the little book of Haggai lacks a general heading, or superscription. It begins immediately with the date, and the names of the people to whom a group of Yahweh oracles are addressed, by way of the prophet. This is the chroniclelike opening of a five-part series of reports, all introduced in more or less the same way: cf. 1:1 with 1:15b—2:2; 2:10, 20f.; on 1:15a see p. 40ff. below. In the light of the language of these introductions, we may call these *accounts of the confronting event of God's word;* cf. היה דבר־יהוה ("the word of Yahweh came") in 1:1; 2:1, 10, 20.

Precise *dating* of the kind we find here (where the very day is noted) is never found anywhere else in prophecy except in Zechariah (1:7; 7:1) and Ezekiel (12 times; cf. W. Zimmerli, *Ezechiel,* BK XIII [1969] 12*ff., 40f.; cf. Eng. *Ezekiel* [1979], 9ff., 72-74, 111-115). In these passages too the dating is almost always associated with the formula for the confronting event of God's word (הוה דבר־ יהוה, "the word of Yahweh came"). Ezekiel's concern here is to pin down or formulate great experiences of revelation—and always in autobiographical style (e.g., 1:1-3; 8:1f.; 33:21; 40:1). In Haggai, on the other hand, the prophet is always talked *about,* in the third person; and the preposition אל ("to"), which generally introduces the prophet as recipient of the word, is used in this book only in 2:10[2] and 20: "the word came *to* Haggai." Otherwise we find the preposition ביד (1:1, 3; 2:1), whereby the prophet is termed the mediator: the word came *through* him. (On אל־חגי, "to Haggai," in 2:10, 20 see pp. 89 and 98f. below.) As here, the writer almost never neglects to add after Haggai's name הנביא, "the prophet" (1:1, 3, 12a; 2:1, 10). The apposition is missing only in 2:13f., 20. On the other hand, personal details—the name of Haggai's father, the place he came from, and the circumstances of the time—are missing altogether: the chronicler either thinks them unimportant, or they are unknown to him. Consequently these first, introductory sentences have a highly official character, the more so since the receivers of the word are presented with their official titles, "governor of Judah" and "high priest." For that reason, and because of the emphatically chronological order of his other accounts, the writer may be called *the Haggai chronicler.*

How long do we continue to hear his voice after v. 1? Verses 2-3 display a strangely transitional character. Verse 2 certainly begins with the messenger formula. But what follows in v. 2b is merely a citation of what the people are saying, and does no more than sound the theme of the later prophetic words (cf. v. 4). But first, v. 3 repeats the formula for the event of God's word. This is never to be found in Haggai's own later prophetic sayings, but it does occur regularly in the introductions of the Haggai chronicler (1:1; 2:1, 10, 20, as also in 1:3). The Haggai sayings themselves are either introduced or completed with the divine-oracle formula (נאם יהוה (צבאות), "saying of Yahweh (Sebaoth)" (1:9), or the messenger formula (כה) אמר יהוה), "(thus) says Yahweh" (1:5, 7, 8). In 1:3, the preposition ביד ("through") and the apposition הנביא ("the prophet"), as well as the formula for the confronting event of God's word, are indications that this is the language of the chronicler.

What does this tell us, or allow us to deduce, about v. 2? The content of vv. 2b and 4 is obviously linked. This shows that the chronicler has taken over 2b from the Haggai saying that had been passed down to him, so as to make known as soon as possible the actual substance of his report to the people who are named in

---

[2] In spite of RSV, which reads: "the word ... came *by* Haggai." MT has אל, "to" (trans.).

v. 1 as being politically and religiously responsible. Together with this anticipation of the beginning of the prophetic words passed down to him, the chronicler may also have taken over the messenger formula in 2a. Thus 2a suggests that 2b has been taken from the prophet's own saying. But in so putting together v. 2 (which works with the material of the prophet's words) the chronicler made v. 3 necessary, as the final transition to the group of actual prophetic oracles; cf. A. S. van der Woude, *Haggai* (1982) 23f. Verses 1-3 in their present form may therefore be assigned to the Haggai chronicler. There is hence no need to deduce thatv. 2 is a reference to some earlier proclamation on Haggai's part (W. Rudolph's postulate: KAT XIII/4, 1976).

A series of prophetic oracles follows in vv. 4-11. This is not a single, self-contained utterance. That is already made plain by the repetition of the formulas used to introduce messenger speeches (5a, 7a, 8b) and divine oracles (9bα), as well as by the change from discussion sayings in interrogative style (4, 9b) with repeated admonitions or exhortations (5b, 7b, 8a) and promises (8b), as well as reminders of the present time of trouble, including special futility curse elements (6, 9a; see pp. 43f. below) and proofs of guilt (9b, 10), in which the present distress is shown to be ultimately the fulfillment of God's word of judgment (v. 11). In 8b, 9 and 11 we find Yahweh's ''I.'' Haggai's ''I'' never appears at all.

Seen as a whole, the utterances must be described as ''composite'' in character (see W. A. M. Beuken, *Haggai ... Studien zur Überlieferungsgeschichte* [1967] 185). The address style is preserved throughout. The different genre elements can best be understood in the context of a *disputation* (see C. Westermann, *ThLZ* 94 [1969] 426). The provocative thesis that it is not the time to build the temple has been anticipated by the chronicler in v. 2b, as background information for the governor and the high priest. The various sayings accordingly go into the question whether the time to rebuild Yahweh's house has nonetheless come (4b, 8a, 9b).

All in all, the structural variety of the sayings and the thematic links between them suggest that the composition we have before us in vv. 4-11 should be understood as *the sketch of a scene* in which the prophet delivers his utterances. Here observations about the transmission of the Hosea oracles may be useful (see H. W. Wolff, BK XIV/1 [Eng., *Hosea*, 1986[4], xxx, 75f., 96, 110ff.]). W. A. M. Beuken has taken up these observations (op. cit., 204ff., 335); cf. also J. W. Whedbee, ''Question-Answer Scheme,'' *Fests. LaSor* [1978] 185f., and D. L. Petersen, *Haggai and Zechariah* [1984] 38f. We may suppose that a disciple or friend (cf. Jer. 8:16; Jer. 36) wrote down and preserved the most striking words uttered by the prophet on a particular occasion. We have no Haggai utterances recorded in the autobiographical ''I,'' as we do in the case of Zechariah. In the series of oracles in the scene-sketches, we may assume that remarks were thrown in here and there by listeners (though they are not recorded) and that these provoked new prophetic sayings. That would explain both the repeated new beginnings (5, 7, 9), as well as the variants of sayings similar in content (6, 9a) and the repetitions (5b, 7b). Unlike the recorder of Hosea's sayings, the Haggai reporter has also noted down a saying of the prophet's listeners at the beginning (2b; see pp. 32f. above), as well as the effect of the prophet's words on them at the end (12b-13). The author of our scene-sketch is clearly distinguishable in both his language and his concern from the prophetic oracles in their spoken form and from the Haggai chronicler.

The chronicler must have taken over the quotation in 2b from what was originally the beginning of the scene-sketch, vv. 4-11, that is to say, he is clearly interested in the attitude of the people. But *the account of the results* is to be found in what is now the continuation of the chapter, in vv. 12-14. This account is not unified, however. It can be shown that only vv. 12b and 13 belonged to the scene-sketch, which the chronicler must already have had in front of him. The reasons for this conclusion would seem to be compelling ones. Verse 12b describes the effect on "the people." Not only do העם ("the people") and לעם ("to the people") in 12b and 13a correspond to העם הזה ("this people") in 2b; the same may be said of the second person plural used throughout the direct-speech sayings, vv. 4-10. Zerubbabel (referred to in 2:2, 4, 21, 23) and Joshua (referred to in 2:2, 4) are not mentioned here at all, any more than they are in 1:12b-13. On the other hand, both 12a and 14 do talk about them, and do so in an unbroken coherence which is not interrupted by vv. 12b-13 but apparently finds its justification in these verses. Verses 12a and 14 correspond exactly to the style of the Haggai chronicler we met in 1:1. Only he now has to talk about "the people" as addressees, as well as Zerubbabel and Joshua, since this is required by the scene-sketch copy he is using (vv. 12b-13). These people, however, are defined more closely as "the remnant of the people" (cf. here pp. 51f. below). Verse 12a calls Haggai "the prophet," as the chronicler does in vv. 1 and 3 as well, whereas the scene-sketch applies the unusual description "the messenger of Yahweh" (v. 13). The official descriptions of Zerubbabel and Joshua, familiar from v. 1, are not lacking in (12a and) 14 either. In v. 13 what we are presuming to be the sketch of a scene, closes with an assurance to the people which corresponds to a later saying in 2:4b. But the Haggai chronicler takes further the story of what resulted, bringing it down to the beginning of work on the temple. What he evidently wants to do from the very beginning is to write a chronicle about the building of the temple.

At the end of v. 14, the Masoretic textual tradition marks the close of the first account of the confronting event of God's word with פ, the sign that represents the close of the *parashah,* or section. One reason alone for not necessarily linking v. 15a with v. 14 is that in the Haggai chronicle the dates otherwise always stand at the beginning of the account of the event of God's word. The present clash of two datings in 1:15a and 1:15b—2:1 makes us ask whether a "word event" is to be found without the introductory date anywhere else in the book of Haggai. It would have to be a saying whose content would explain the present position of 1:15a after 1:14. For a solution of the problem see pp. 59ff. below.

According to our observations hitherto, three different types of text anteceded the secondary, or later, assignment of 1:15a to 1:14—an assignment which was made in the final editing process: (1) the sayings of the prophet Haggai himself, delivered in *the disputation* (4, 5f., 7f., 9-11); (2) the prophetic sayings or oracles (vv. 4-11) preserved in writing by one of the prophet's pupils or disciples in *the scene-sketches,* these including a description of the situation (2b) and the account of the results (12b-13); (3) *the Haggai chronicle,* which worked in the scene sketches and developed them into a first full-scale account of the confronting event of God's word.

Setting

When and where did the three versions come into being? Nothing speaks against a date for the prophetic sayings themselves in accordance with the chronicler's introduction (v. 1): the first day of the sixth month in the second year of the reign of Darius I—i.e., August 29, 520. (The calculation here and below follows R. A. Parker and W. H. Dubberstein, *Babylonian Chronology* [1956].) It is the height of the summer. The damage resulting from the unusual drought of the preceding year (or even years) are making themselves felt (6, 9-11). The disputation may have taken place in the immediate environs of the ruined temple, so that a pointing finger made plain what was meant by "this house" (v. 4b). An assembly place for prayer and sacrifice will have been provisionally set up near the temple ruins: Jer. 41:5; Zech. 7:3, 5; 8:19; and Ezra 3:2f. all presuppose this; cf. Hag. 2:14b and p. 94 below (also M. Noth, *Geschichte Israels* [1969[7]] 263; Eng. trans. of 2nd ed. of 1954, *History of Israel,* 1960[2]).

It is uncertain whether the written record of the prophet's words (4-11) was already made on the actual day of their proclamation, if indeed we are correct in thinking that a brief report on their result (12b) and a short prophetic assurance (13) belong to this first scene-sketch.

The chronicler's report developed in vv. 1-3 and 12a, 14 could have originated at the earliest after the date of the last account of the confronting event of God's word (2:10, 20)—that is to say, after December 18, 520—if we could be certain that all the chronicler's reports were written down at the same time; though this is suggested by the great unity of language. But even where the language is concerned, the possibility of two phases is worth consideration; see p. 99 below. The scene on the 21st day of the 7th month of the 2nd year of Darius's reign (1:15b—2:1 = October 17, 520), like our first scene (1:1), is dated in the following order: year—month—day. Haggai is introduced in 1:1 as the mediator of the word (בְּיַד, "through"). (On 1:15a see pp. 59f. below.) On the other hand, the first saying belonging to the 24th day of the 9th month of the 2nd year of Darius's reign (2:10 = December 18, 520) is dated in the order: day—month—year. The second saying belonging to the same day (2:20) repeats only the day and the month. If, now, the introductions to the accounts of the 1st day of the 6th month (August 29) and the 21st day of the 7th month (= October 17)—i.e., 1:1 and 1:15b—2:1 together with the original text of 1:15a, with its pointer to the 24th day of the 6th month = September 21—were formulated *before* the 24th day of the 9th month (= December 18), then three other minor differences in the language of this chronicle could be more easily explained: (a) that Haggai is presented in 2:10 and 20 as

35

the recipient of the word (אֶל, "to") and no longer, as in 1:1, 3; 2:1, as its mediator (בְּיַד "through"); (b) that the apposition הַנָּבִא ("the prophet") is missing in 2:20 for the only time in the Haggai chronicle (but cf. pp. 98f. below)); and finally (c) that in 2:23 we find the phrase "on that day," which is the formula used as a link between oracles—its one and only occurrence in the book of Haggai. There is no absolutely compelling evidence for distinguishing two phases in the genesis of the building chronicle, but the possibility is worth bearing in mind, in the context of other observations. If we were to accept it, the first account, 1:1-14, together with the second indicated in 1:15a (2:15-19; see p. 61 below), as well as the third account, transmitted in 1:15b-2:9, would all have originated after the 21st day of the 7th month (= October 17) and before the 24th day of the 9th month (= December 18)—that is to say, before Zechariah's first appearance in the 8th month (Zech. 1:1). The report would then be a memorandum of the first steps in the reconstruction of the temple—unless indeed the redaction of the Haggai chronicler should after all be viewed as a unity, in the light of the decisions about 2:14 and 23 (see pp. 52f. and 108 below).

Commentary

[1:1]   Haggai's whole proclamation is set by his chronicler in a worldwide context, in a way unparalleled in any earlier prophetic book; cf.—in addition to 1:1— 1:15b; 2:10. Darius I is quite simply called "the king" (Old Iranian: *dârayatwahuš* = "he who sustains the good"; Persian: *dâreyawôš;* Greek: Δαρεῖος). The son of Hystaspes, Darius belonged to a collateral branch of the Achaemenid family. After the death of Cyrus's son Cambyses (529–522), who had already had his brother Bardiya (Greek: Smerdis) murdered about 526, Darius was finally able to establish himself in the face of usurpers such as Gaumâta, though only after long-drawn-out conflicts about the succession (see pp. 75f. below). He reigned from 522/21 to 486/85; cf. *Reallexikon der Assyriologie* (1932ff.) II, 121f.; *Der kleine Pauly: Lexikon der Antike,* ed. K. Ziegler and W. Sontheimer (1964–75) I, 1390f.; R. Borger, *Chronologie des Darius-Denkmals...* NAWG (1982) 103-132. By the second year of Darius's reign, Judah was firmly in the hands of the Persian king, even if tremors still made themselves felt elsewhere in the empire, as the aftermath of the succession conflicts.

According to our chronology, *the date* of Haggai's appearance on the scene on the first day of the sixth month in the second year of Darius's reign corresponds to August 29, 520 B.C. (calculation according to R. A. Parker and W. H. Dubberstein, *Babylonian Chronology* [1956] 15-17). Since the year began in the spring, the sixth month started at the end of August, in Israel too (at latest from the end of the exile; cf. M. Weippert, "Kalender und Zeitrechnung," *Biblisches Reallexikon,* ed. K. Galling [1977²] 167f.). It was still the hottest time of the year. Perhaps the first day of the month offered a special opportunity for meeting together, if the new moon was celebrated with sacrificial rites in the area of the sanctuary; cf. Amos 8:5; 2 Kings 4:23 with Ezek. 45:17; 1 Chron. 23:31; 2 Chron. 31:3

and especially Ezra 3:(1-)6; on the lunar month calculation, cf. M. Weippert, op. cit., 166f.

The actual event which the Haggai chronicler has to report, and which dominates everything that follows, is *the going forth of a word, or oracle, from Yahweh.* For a messenger of God to be seized by the word was a confronting event that again and again determined Israel's history. This was manifested in the sixth century especially by the phrase היה דבר־יהוה, "the word of Yahweh came," which we find preeminently in the Deuteronomic history and in the books of Jeremiah and Ezekiel (where it occurs 12, 30, and 50 times, respectively; cf. BK XIV/1, 2 (Eng. *Hosea* [1986⁴] 3). Whereas the phrase generally introduces the prophet *as recipient* of Yahweh's word, by way of the preposition אל ("to"), here this preposition is used so that the stress falls on Zerubbabel and Joshua as the actual addressees, while the prophet recedes into the background as *mediator* of the word (ביד = intensified ב-*instrumentalis,* "through"; cf. Hos. 12:11b with Hos. 1:2a and b). ביד as preposition seldom occurs in older texts (1 Sam. 28:15, 17; Hos. 12:11). It becomes more frequent only in the typically Deuteronomistic sections of the books of Kings (1 Kings 12:15; 15:29; 16:12, 34; 17:16; 2 Kings 9:36; 14:25; 17:13, 23; 21:10 and frequently). In the Chronicler's history the phrase בְּיַד משׁה for example ("through Moses") is quite common (2 Chron. 33:8; 34:14; 35:6 and frequently), just as it is in the priestly writing (Exod. 9:35; 35:29; Lev. 8:36 and frequently); cf. W. A. M. Beuken, op. cit., 28, and R. A. Mason, "Editorial Framework" (1977), 415. This does not allow us to deduce any direct influence on the Haggai chronicler, however. He is simply writing in the tradition that ran from the Deuteronomic writings to the Chronicler.

The mediator of Yahweh's word here is called *Haggai.* The name is mentioned nine times in the two chapters of this building chronicle, and twice in the book of Ezra (5:1; 6:14), where Haggai is mentioned before Zechariah (just as he comes before Zechariah in the order of the Book of the Twelve Prophets). This clearly has chronological reasons (cf. Hag. 1:1 with Zech. 1:1). In the Old Testament world, we find evidence of the name on Hebrew seals, as well as in Phoenician and South Arabian texts (A. S. van der Woude, *Haggai* [1982] 9); but it is particularly frequent in Aramaic sources (cf. A. Cowley, *Aramaic Papyri of the 5th Century B.C.* [1923] 286). The name was so popular and widespread because it is an allusion to the birth on a feast day of the person so named (חַג). This counted as a good omen. The Hebrew sounds like "my feast day's joy!"; cf. שַׁבְּתַי, "the one born on the sabbath" (Ezra 10:15; Neh. 8:7; 11:16) and our "Sunday's child" (M. Noth, *Die israelitischen Personennamen im Rahmen der gemeinsemitischen Namengebung,* BWANT 46 [1928] 222). For Akkadian and Egyptian parallels, see J. J. Stamm, *Beiträge zu hebräischen und altorientalischen Namenskunde* [1980] 118f.). The Septuagint's version of the name is Ἀγγαῖος, the Vulgate's *Agg(a)eus.*

Haggai is presented by his chronicler as *"the prophet"* (as in 1:1 so also in 1:3, 12; 2:1, 10; cf. also Ezra 5:1; 6:14). This is a way of stressing that he had a special mission. It does not mean that he should be regarded as a "cultic prophet,"

and that his zeal for the rebuilding of the temple should be viewed in that light (thus
J. Blenkinsopp, *A History of Prophecy in Israel* [1983] 232; for a different view,
cf. R. R. Wilson, *Prophecy and Society in Ancient Israel* [1980] 287f.). His ardent
future expectation alone would place him outside these narrow confines (2:6ff.,
21ff.). He deals with priestly questions like a person strange to them (2:11-13). On
the other hand, he addresses the high priest with as much assurance, and as much
success, as he does the political governor (2:4; cf. 1:12 and G. Sauer, *Serubbabel
in der Sicht Haggais und Sacharjas*, BZAW 105 [1967] 206).

Haggai therefore impressed his chronicler and the postexilic community
as a prophet of extraordinary authority, whose critical energy, fired by his confidence, led to success (1:14; Ezra 5:1f.; 6:14). It may be significant that the putative
author of the first scene-sketch gives him the unusual title "messenger of Yahweh"
(1:13; see pp. 49f. below). Probably Haggai was not himself one of the exiles who
had returned home a short time previously, since his name is not mentioned in the
list given in Ezra 2. He never seems to remember the exile (unlike Zechariah:
1:14ff.; 2:6ff.; 6:15). We should more probably assign him to the group of old
Judaeans who had never been deported and who lived as עַם הָאָרֶץ ("people of the
land," 2:4aβ) in the towns of Judah (see pp. 40 and 51 below on 1:2 and 12a; for
the discussion cf. K. Galling, *Studien* [1964] 116f.). It is curious that he never
mentions the city of Jerusalem or Zion, apart from the temple, but he is evidently
familiar with an agricultural milieu (1:6, 8, 9; 2:16; see here W. A. M. Beuken,
Haggai ... Studien [1967] 216-229, 334). In this respect he is quite unlike
Zechariah (1:14, 16; 2:2, 4, 7, 10; 3:2; 8:2-5). Cf. p. 79 below.

But the Haggai chronicler is evidently not interested in telling us whether
Haggai was one of the homecomers or one of the old Judaeans. The important thing
for him is that Haggai is the mediator of Yahweh's word, and that it should reach
Zerubbabel and Joshua. Nor does he mention that both these men were themselves
among those who had recently returned from exile, though we know from the name
list in Ezra 2:1f. that this was the fact (cf. also Neh. 7:5, 7). We in any case know
that Zerubbabel was one of the exiles because of the Akkadian origin of his name:
Zēr-Bābili means "offshoot of Babylon." Since he was the son of Shealtiel, we
must suppose that he was a grandson, born in exile, of the Davidic king Jehoiachin.
His grandfather was deported from Jerusalem to Babylon when he was 18 years old
(2 Kings 24:8, 15). According to the Masoretic text of 1 Chron. 3:17-19, however,
Zerubbabel was one of the sons of Pedaiah, a brother of Shealtiel's. The Septuagint
text of 1 Chron. 3:19 offers us Shealtiel instead of Pediah, like Hag. 1:1 and Ezra
3:2; 5:2. As a solution of this problem W. Rudolph suggests a levirate marriage
(Deut. 25:5ff.; cf. his commentary to Ezra and Nehemiah, HAT I/20 [1949] 18f.).
For a critical comment on this view see S. Japhet, "Sheshbazzar and Zerubbabel,"
ZAW (1982) 71ff.

Although the Haggai chronicler does not mention that Zerubbabel was
born in exile, he finds his present function as פחת יהודה (Persian) governor of
Judah, very important indeed; cf. also 1:14; 2:2, 21.

Excursus: The Persian Administrative System

If the official title פֶּחָה, *pechah*, were to be used rather loosely, it could be the term used for a "repatriation commissioner" (A. Alt, *Kleine Schriften* II [1963³] 333-337; KBL³ 872b) on whom special powers for Judah had been conferred, but who would have been subject, under constitutional law, to the provincial governor in Samaria; cf. K. Galling, *Studien* (1964) 135; S. Herrmann, *Theologische Realenzyklopädie* (1976–) 12,725, lines 25ff. More recent epigraphical material, however (N. Avigad, *Qedem* 4 [1976] 32-36), makes it seem more probable that Judah should be viewed as already a separate province (separate, that is, from Samaria) in Haggai's time, not just in Nehemiah's (Neh. 5:14 cj.). This means that פחה, *pechah,* should be understood as the precise designation for the governor (S. Japhet, 80ff.), especially since the connected phrase פחת יהודה ("governor of Judah") is established usage in Haggai, as the repetition shows (1:1, 14; 2:2, 21; cf., as long ago as 1952, F. M. Heidelheim, *Handbuch der Orientalistik*, ed. B. Spuler, I/2.4.2, 102).

The official designation פחה was used for the chief administrative officer of administrative districts, both large and small. Judah was one of the smaller provinces, on a level with the provinces of Samaria, Galilee, Idumaea, and others. As פחת יהודה, Zerubbabel was the chief administrative officer for Judah, like Sheshbazzar before him, Sheshbazzar having been appointed פחה by Cyrus, according to Ezra 5:14. The smaller Palestinian and Syrian provinces were, as a trans-Euphrates region (Ezra 5:3), under the jurisdiction of the satrapy whose Aramaic name was *Abarnahara* (Babylonian: *Ebirnari*). The administrative center of the satrapy was Damascus; and its governor (פחה) Tattenai is mentioned in Ezra 5:3, 6; 6:6, 13 as being responsible for Judah too. Tattenai himself, together with the administrator of the area between the Euphrates and the Tigris, was subject to the governor of Babylon and Abarnahara, whose seat was in Babylon. It is only in the case of these higher civil servants that we should use the title *satrap*. It may therefore no doubt be properly applied to the פחה of Abarnahara, Tattenai. But it is not the appropriate title for the פחה of Judah or Samaria. Cf. O. Leuze, *Die Satrapieneinteilung ...* (1935) 36-42.

The Haggai chronicler therefore introduces the Davidic Zerubbabel in his official function as Persian "governor of Judah." In the list of homecomers in Ezra 2:1f. (= Neh. 7:7) Zerubbabel heads a leading group of 12 (elders) and a large number of other returning exiles—40,000 in all, according to Ezra 2:64.

In Ezra 2:2, as here in Haggai, the high priest Joshua is put side by side with Zerubbabel. יְהוֹשֻׁעַ ("Joshua") is the first name in the history of Israel to have been formed from the name *Yahweh: Joshua* means "Yahweh is help." In Ezra 2:2 and again in 3:2, 8; 5:2; Neh. 7:7 the name appears in the variant יֵשׁוּעַ, "Jeshua" (Noth, *Personennamen,* op. cit.: vocalic dissimilation). The context makes it certain that there too the high priest mentioned in the book of Haggai is meant. We need only look at Ezra 2:2; 3:8; 5:2. That Joshua too came from the gola is clearly confirmed by the mention of his father Jehozadak who, according to 1 Chron. 6:15, was deported by Nebuchadnezzar. According to 2 Kings 25:18, his grandfather Seraiah (1 Chron. 6:14) was taken captive in 587 as "chief priest" and was executed in Riblah (2 Kings 25:18, 21). Thus Joshua ben Jehozadak belonged within the succession of the Levitical priests and the Zadokites (1 Chron. 6:1-15). After his grandfather had been named הַכֹּבֵן הָרֹאשׁ, "head priest," Joshua was, as far as we know, the first of the "top" priests to bear the title הַכֹּהֵן הַגָּדוֹל, "the chief priest." It was probably only subsequently, in postexilic times, that the title was applied to Jehoiada and Hilkiah in 2 Kings 12:10; 22:4, 8; 23:4.

Whereas the governor of Judah disposed over the work force for the rebuilding of the temple, the high priest required the temple particularly for his special services. He had to perform sacrifices on the altar for burnt offerings, and he alone was permitted to enter the Holy of Holies, for the reconciliation of the whole congregation (Lev.16).

It is noticeable that in v. 1 the people are not mentioned as being recipients of the prophet's word, in addition to the governor and the high priest, even though the oracles in vv. 4-11 seem to be addressed to the people (v. 2), and even though later, in 12a and 12b-13, the people are also explicitly named as listeners, as well as Zerubbabel and Joshua. This means that it is not enough to say that in the ancient Near East temple-building was in general a government affair, and that in the Chronicler's history special prophetic sayings are addressed to kings (2 Chron. 12:5; 15:1f.), to whom Zerubbabel has now succeeded. The continuation of the introduction in v. 2 shows rather that the prophet is not initially regarding the people as listeners at all; he is placing them before the governor and the high priest as accused.

[1:2]   The Haggai chronicler does this by citing from the prophetic scene-sketch (see pp. 33f. above) the classic messenger formula (''thus has Yahweh of hosts spoken'' cf. vv. 5, 7), as a reminder of the prophet's report in his function as Yahweh's messenger. Here, as generally in the messenger formula, אמר should be translated by the perfect tense (''has said''), not by the present (cf. H. W. Wolff, BK XIV/2, 165f. [Eng., *Joel and Amos*, 1985[3], 135ff.]). This view is supported by K. Elliger, *Deuterojesaja*, BK XI (1978), 464f., contrary to A. J. Bjørndalen, ''Zu den Zeitstufen der Zitatformel ... כֹּה אָמַר im Botenverkehr,'' ZAW 86 (1974) 393-403.

As indictment arising from the disputation, the chronicler first puts forward the protest of ''this people here.'' This makes it clear why the people is not named as addressee in v. 1. The responsible leaders of the community have to decide between the people and the prophet, and must initiate the appropriate steps, in line with Haggai's purpose. העם הזה, ''this people here,'' is an expression of displeasure and rejection. It points to guilt and judgment (cf. 2:14; Zech. 8:11; Isa. 6:9f.; 8:6, 12; Jer. 4:11, and frequently elsewhere; cf. also in the New Testament ἡ γενεὰ αὕτη, ''this generation,'' Matt. 23:36; Mark 8:38; Luke 11:30, 50f.; 17:25). Who is meant by ''this people''? Old established Judaeans who had never been deported? Or homecomers from the gola, who had only recently returned with Zerubbabel and Joshua? The governor and the high priest are responsible for both national groups. It is only in 12a and 14 that the Haggai chronicler suggests for the first time that he is thinking primarily of the homecomers (see pp. 51f. below). But there is no indication that Haggai himself intended to exclude the old Judaeans, to whom he himself probably belonged.

''This people here'' is indicted because it does not see that the time to rebuild the temple has now come. ''Yahweh's house'' is Haggai's leitmotif, his whole theme. The rebuilding had been an open question for 18 years. The restoration of the temple was the object of Cyrus's edict of 538 (Ezra 6:3-5; cf. Ezra 1:2-4). A first attempt to rebuild it under Sheshbazzar in 537 (cf. Ezra 1:7-11 and 5:14-16)—an attempt later ascribed to Zerubbabel—soon came to a standstill (Ezra 4:24; cf. W. Rudolph, KAT XIII/4 [1976] 33). Now Haggai has apparently once more called, in the name of his God, for the work to begin. This is the premise of the protest cited in Hag. 1:2b.

Why do the people think that the time has not yet come? Are they inhibited for theological reasons? This will have to emerge from the following disputation. Did people believe that the time of curse, which reached its climax with the destruction of the temple in 587, had not yet run its full course (cf. Zech. 1:12)? Did they have to wait to build the temple until the time of salvation had manifestly dawned, and for the coming of the Messiah? Cf. J. Wellhausen, *Die kleine Propheten* (1892, 1963⁴) 173; E. Janssen, *Juda in der Exilszeit* (1956) 78; O. H. Steck, *ZAW* 83 (1971) 373ff. It is indirectly at most that Haggai combats views of this kind. The sayings in vv. 4-11 suggest rather that the people did not feel they were in a position to rebuild because of their wretched economic situation.

[1:3] With v. 3 the chronicler leads over to the words of the prophetic scene-sketch. The transitional passage in v. 3 still conforms entirely to the style of the Haggai chronicler, which is characterized by the formula for the confronting event of God's word and by the designation of Haggai as mediator of the word (ביד, "through") and as "the prophet" (see p. 32 above). The formula for the event of God's word in v. 3 ("the word of Yahweh went out") is not intended to be taken literally before v. 2b, any more than the messenger formula in 2a ("Thus has Yahweh of hosts spoken"), for the following verse (4) says "Yahweh's house" and not "my house." This disharmony becomes comprehensible if with v. 3 the chronicler is leading over to the prophetic oracle which is already in the copy from which he is working. He makes no distinction between the words of the prophet and Yahweh's word.

[1:4] Verse 4 draws us immediately into an extremely lively dispute. The presupposition may perhaps be an earlier call by Haggai for the temple to be rebuilt (though this has not been passed down to us)—a call that had been rejected by the people (v. 2b). The prophet picks up, quite literally, the people's assertion that the time for Yahweh's house has not yet come. As is typical of classical prophecy, in his confutation Haggai goes into the actual words of his hearers. With a thrice-repeated, emphatic address (לכם אתם...בבתיכם; cf. textual note 4a) and in a challenging, cynical, interrogative style, he shows up their egoism for what it is. And in so doing he goes straight as a die for his real theme, by contrasting "this house" of Yahweh's with the houses of his listeners. What is time there for? The question of obedience is presented as a question about priorities: to what does one give priority in allotting one's time? Cf. E. Jenni, "עת - Zeit," *THAT* II, 370-385. Haggai puts this question to people who are exerting their energies for their own "dwelling." Does שֵׁבֶת, "dwell," indicate an already achieved permanent condition? We could then deduce from the formulation that the people concerned were (exclusively) old Judaeans, who possessed houses that were already complete (O. H. Steck). Or can the infinitive construction לְשֶׁבֶת, "to dwell," describe the desired goal, so that we might also think of the homecomers, who were only now in the process of "setting up house" (cf. 9bγ)?

This double question is connected with the problem of how to interpret the houses as סְפוּנִים. סָפַן as a specialized architectural term is otherwise found in the Old Testament only in reports about the building of the temple (1 Kings 6:9) or of royal palaces (1 Kings 7:3, 7; Jer. 22:14). In these contexts the use of costly cedarwood is always mentioned. Does this not therefore mean that we should interpret סָפַן as "panel"? But cedarwood is also necessary for the roofing of large rooms, because it provides sufficiently long beams. Thus in 1 Kings 6:9; 7:3 סָפַן is used in connection with the roofing of temples and palaces (cf. M. Noth, *Könige 1–16*, BK IX/1 (1983²) on this passage; also p. 137). If it were a matter of flat roofs belonging to ordinary houses, the local sycamores, which were much smaller, could have been used (K. Galling and H. Rösel, "Dach," *BRL²* 54). So when Haggai is speaking about the houses of the people, in reading סָפֻן, passive participle, we shall have to think of the simple roofing necessary to make a house inhabitable at all. Haggai is talking about what is necessary, not what is luxurious. Roofed-in houses "to live in" (לְשֶׁבֶת) are needed by both the old Judaeans and the homecomers from the gola. (If, instead of the meaning adopted here, we nonetheless wished to think of paneled walls in connection with סָפַן, we should have to interpret the question in an ironic sense, as S. Amsler does [CAT XIc (1981)]. Haggai would then be addressing his listeners as people who were equipping their own houses in the princely fashion otherwise enjoyed only by the temple and by royal palaces.)

Haggai contrasts "this house here" with the houses of the people, which are fit to live in. He points to the heap of rubble. He calls it חָרֵב, meaning "the final stage of a devastation" (K. Galling, *Studien* [1964] 128; KBL³ 335: "waste" or "desolate"). We have to imagine the dimensions of the ruins. The central building of the temple burned down in 587 (2 Kings 25:8ff.) was 100 ft. long, about 30 ft. wide and 50 ft. high. The vestibule was 5 times 30 ft. (or 5 times 45 ft.?), the Holy of Holies 30 ft. by 30 ft. by 30 ft.; cf. 1 Kings 6:2ff. and M. Noth, *Könige 1–16*, BK IX, (1983²) 110f.; A. Kuschke, "Tempel," *BRL²* 338-341. The field of ruins was correspondingly huge. All the wooden parts had been razed to the ground. Apart from the wooden cube of the Holy of Holies (1 Kings 6:16, 20a), this included the wall paneling (Ezra 5:8f.), the flat roof, which was made of cedar beams, and—at the sides—a layer of wooden beams supported by three layers of rectangular stone blocks (1 Kings 6:36; cf. Ezra 5:8; 6:4; 1 Kings 7:12); see here T. A. Busink, *Der Tempel* (1980) 807-809: "stone structure with wooden grids" (as a protection against earthquakes). On these then rested the walls, which were made of sun-dried clay bricks, a good six feet thick (K. Galling, *Studien,* 129; M. Noth, BK IX, 128). When the wooden sections burned, these walls collapsed; even the stone blocks broke apart. The winter rains of almost 70 years completed the work of destruction. Soon after 587 the lamentation was already heard that "Mount Zion lies desolate; jackals prowl over it" (Lam. 5:18). Haggai points out this mountain of ruins to people who have time only for their own houses. It is hardly possible to recognize that this was Yahweh's house. Zechariah calls the place of ruins a "great mountain" (4:7). But it must still have been recognizably the ruins of the temple; otherwise the comparison with the earlier temple in 2:3 would be pointless (T. A. Busink, op. cit., 776).

[1:5] How does Haggai go about persuading the people to begin rebuilding? What he now says is said as Yahweh's messenger (v. 5a). Between the time for their own houses and the time for Yahweh's house, he decides what has to be done "now" for God's sake. The beginning should be made *now,* immediately, in the very hour when his words are heard. He starts out with a demand unusual in prophecy but reminiscent of Deuteronomic and wisdom admonitions: "Focus your heart on your ways!" לְבַב, though usually translated "heart," is here the organ that makes spiritual and mental perception possible; cf. Deut. 29:4 and H. W. Wolff, *Anthropologie des Alten Testaments* (1973, 1984[4]) 77ff. [Eng., *Anthropology of the Old Testament* (1974), 46ff.]; F. Stolz, *THAT* I, 862f. It is in the heart that critical judgment and the power of proper discernment come about (1 Kings 3:9)—more precisely, in Haggai's context, the power of discerning the times (Isa. 41:22; cf. also Hag. 2:15, 18); for what is at issue here is insight into what is due "now." On what should the heart be focused (שִׂים)—that is to say, reflection and reasoning, and complete, thoughtful attention? It should be focused "on your ways!" Here "the ways" are not Yahweh's commandments (Deut. 31:29; Hos. 14:9; Ps. 18:21 and H. W. Wolff, BK XIV/1 [1976[3]], 310f.; Eng., *Hosea* [1986[4]], 239f., or wisdom (Prov. 4:11)—not even human destinies as such (Isa. 56:11 and K. Koch, "דרך," *ThWAT* II, 307ff.). What is meant is the interaction between behavior and success. Here the דרכים of human beings is a term that brings under a single heading—reduces to a single concept—the way a person takes and the goal that he thereby achieves. The word "ways" in this context therefore corresponds more or less accurately to "how we fare." Haggai's people is now asked to consider the connection between what it has done hitherto and the miseries of its present situation.

[1:6] This is specifically explained in v. 6. Taking up traditional "curse" series, the prophet challenges the people to think about what they have done and what has happened to them. In five sentences he picks up a particular genre, the futility curses; cf. D. R. Hillers, "Treaty Curses and the Old Testament Prophets," *BibOr* 16 (1964) 28f.: ("'Futility' Curses") and H. W. Wolff, *Micha,* XIV/4 (1982) 162, 169ff. These curses, couched in the form of direct address, adduce in the first term vitally important activities, whose hoped-for results are negated in a second term in the form of a curse, generally with וְלֹא, "and not." We have numerous examples of this form of curse from the 8th century B.C., both in Israel and elsewhere;

cf. also W. A. M. Beuken, *Studien,* 190ff. Individual prophetic threats take up
these curses in their strict form; later they are more frequently found in long series
of curses (Lev. 26 and Deut.28). As vitally important activities which have remained ineffective, Haggai names: *sowing* (as Mic. 6:15aα; Lev. 26:16b; Deut.
28:38); *eating* (as Hos. 4:10aα; Mic. 6:14aα; Lev. 26:26b); *drinking* (as Amos
5:11b; Mic. 6:15bβ; Deut. 28:39); *clothing oneself* (otherwise only in a different
form, as Deut. 28:48); and *working for a wage.* These last two activities are not to
be found in the other series of curses known to us. Haggai's independence is also
shown in the fact that instead of the usual negation וְלֹא he thrice opens the second
term of the statement with the intensifying וְאֵין, which includes the idea of "not
being." The essential difference from the other series of curses, however, is to be
seen in the fact that in Haggai the experiences of frustration are not threatened as a
future evil (in the event that a contract be broken, or in the case of disobedience
towards Yahweh). These frustrations are already a fact, and are put forward for
consideration accordingly. This is the way in which we have to understand the
perfect זְרַעְתֶּם (where the tense establishes the fact) and the following stressed absolute infinitives (as well as the participle in b) which are deviations from the imperfect forms used in the comparable texts. Haggai's oracle must therefore be
termed a "curse fulfillment" saying (like Hos. 4:10a). The later-proclaimed blessing (2:19b) is therefore preceded here by reflection about present experiences of
curse.

It will not be by chance that Haggai begins with the seedtime which has
produced so little (cf. 1:9; 2:16). A great drought (1:10f.) with succeeding periods
of hunger and thirst, and also lack of clothing, will have been the decisive common
experience. All the wage earners will have suffered especially from the resulting
high prices. They had to live from wages paid by the day. It is as if the "bag" they
carried on their belts as "purse" (Gen. 42:35; Prov. 7:20; cf. H. Weippert, *BRL²*,
89) were full of holes, "perforated" (נקב—passive participle *qal*). The money they
have saved disappears because its purchasing power falls as prices soar (cf. also
Mal. 3:5). Working for wages therefore shows itself to be just as futile as sowing,
eating, drinking, and clothing oneself.

If the wretched situation described in these five sentences is considered as
a whole, it would seem improbable that Haggai is pointing merely to "the spring
and summer of 520" and means "the drought of 520 especially" (K. Galling's
view: *Studien,* 57); for the rainy season falls in the months of November to April,
whereas from May to October there is never much rain at any time; cf. G. Dalman,
Arbeit und Sitte in Palästina I/1 (1937) 36ff. At the end of August 520 the prophet
will probably have been thinking of more than a single catastrophic year,
particulary so since he is thinking, not only of food, but also of clothing and of high
prices in general, which are influenced by drought in the long term, especially if
the rains fail for more than one year in succession. At all events, the prophet urges
the people to think about effort and (insufficient) results, achievement and ill success. By reshaping the traditional futility curses into curse-fulfillment sayings—
i.e., into a situation analysis—he lays bare the wrongness of what the people are

doing, concerned as they are, not with Yahweh's house, but only with their own lives—and in vain.

[1:7] Perhaps his admonition triggered off a lively discussion. Beginning to speak afresh—and this time explicitly presenting what he says as Yahweh's word (7a)—the prophet (or the author of the scene-sketch) repeats his admonition to the people: they should think about the way they are faring at present (7b, cf. 5).

[1:8] But now he calls them to new action (8a), which is linked with promise (8b).

He names only the first essential steps. "The hills" into which he tells them to go will have been the hilly Judaean countryside round about. In Haggai's time these hills were still thickly wooded, as far as the king's own forests (Neh. 2:8; 8:15f.; cf. Dalman, *Arbeit und Sitte,* I, 76f.). What he has in mind are not the cedars of Lebanon (though cf. Ezra 3:7), but rather the more easily accessible wood: firs, palm trees—perhaps also oaks, poplars, cypresses, sycamores, and olive trees (cf. K. Galling, "Wald und Forstwirtschaft," *BRL*[2] 356-358). All kinds of wood could be used for the layer of beams which served as stabilizing building component above the three foundational layers of stone blocks, and beneath the clay-brick walls (Ezra 6:4; see p. 42 above). Wood had to be selected for tools, and above all for the scaffolding. Finally, long, costly beams were needed for the roof, and boards for the inside paneling of the walls. So, since many different kinds of wood had to be fetched, everyone could lend a hand somewhere or other. Stones are not mentioned. Stones there were enough, in and round about the ruins, for the beginning at least: cf. T. A. Busink, *Tempel,* 808. Experts of all kinds for particular work will have been required, but Haggai's call, "Build the house!" embraces the whole people. Just because of that, he puts the call to bring in wood at the very beginning.

Even the smallest beginnings will be sustained by a double promise (8b). First of all, Yahweh himself promises his recognition: וְאֶרְצֶה־בּוֹ. The word רצה often introduces the (factual) object with בְ (Ezek. 20:41; Mic. 6:7; 1 Chron. 28:4); the relationship is thereby intensified. The suffix in בּוֹ is related to בַּיִת ("house") in 8a. The house that is to be built stands from the beginning under the promise that Yahweh will "accept" it (this is the basic meaning of רצה according to G. Gerleman, "רצה—Gefallen haben," *THAT* II, 810-813). The word is primarily a term in cultic law, used by the priest to signify recognition of the legitimacy of what has been brought for sacrifice (Lev. 7:18; 19:7; 22:23; Hos. 8:13; Amos 5:22; Mic. 6:7; cf. H. W. Wolff, BK XIV/1, 186. [Eng., *Hosea,* 1986[4], 144ff]; BK XIV/2, 307 [Eng., *Joel and Amos,* 1985[3], 263]; *Micha,* XIV/4 (1982), 151f.). In these contexts it is the priest who takes up Yahweh's "I"; here it is the prophet. But whereas the priestly "recognition" applies to the visibly presented sacrifice, the prophet expresses the future joyful acceptance of the temple building, which has not yet even been begun—expresses it as if the building had already been impeccably completed. He already sets even the very first beginnings in the light of the promise.

The second assurance goes further still. The shorter imperfect form וְאֶכָּבֵד (*Ketibh*) is to be preferred to וְאֶכָּבְדָה (*Qere*), which must be understood in a cohortative sense (see textual note to v. 8b above). כבד *niphal* is often passive (''to be honored'') or reflexive-permissive (''to see oneself honored''). But here the promissory character of the statement is brought out better by the translation: ''I will show myself in my glory'' (KBL³ 434). This meaning is frequently found in the wider context to which Haggai belongs, following the priestly writing (Exod. 14:4, 17f.; Lev. 10:3). In Ezek. 28:22; 39:13 it is used towards enemies; in Isa. 26:15 (see H. Wildberger, *Jesaja 13ff*, BK X/2 [1978] textual note to 26:15a) and Isa. 66:5 Gk (*Biblia Hebraica Suttgartensia*) in Israelite context. Here in Haggai the saying promises the people who are getting ready to build the temple, not only its acceptance as Yahweh's house, but also the manifestation of that acceptance through God's presence, power, and compassion. The content of this assurance must be understood in Haggai's sense and in the light of the later promises of salvation (2:9b), blessing (2:19), and peace (2:22) (cf. C. Westermann, ''כבד— schwer sein,'' *THAT* I, 801; P. Stenmans, ''כָּבֵד,'' *ThWAT* IV, 21). Those who have discovered that their self-seeking is in vain (v. 6) will experience through the work they put into Yahweh's house the ''weight'' (כבד = ''to be heavy'') of his presence. Haggai does not press for the temple to be rebuilt in order that the priestly cult may function. The purpose is ''so that Yahweh may enter into it, and may appear for the salvation of the people'' (K. M. Beyse, ''Serubbabel und die Königserwartungen der Propheten Haggai und Zacharja,'' *Arbeiten zur Theologie* I/48 [1972] 65). At the end, the promise that is linked with the admonition is once more (cf. v. 7a) expressly designated as Yahweh's own offer (''thus has Yahweh spoken'').

[1:9] In what follows we undoubtedly still (as in 8b) hear Yahweh's own ''I'' (9aβ, b, 11a). But what is said reverts to the situation analysis. Listeners' interruptions may have been the reason, if we are right in supposing that this is the sketch of a scene in which Haggai addresses the people (see p. 34 above). The very first sentence picks up catchwords from v. 6, and also modifies the style of the futility curses (instead of the announcement in the imperfect tense, the perfect is used, to establish the fact of the fulfillment; see p. 44 above). פנה אל, however, does not, like the preceding sentences in v. 6 (which also have three absolute infinitives) mean a variety of activity (the view taken by K. Elliger and KBL³, 885: ''vieles unternehmen''—''undertake a great deal''). In the light of the basic meaning ''to turn to,'' it more probably means ''to expect much'' (KBL¹, 765). So in 9a we should think in terms of a summing up of the disappointed activities of v.6. ''The little'' that was left was brought ''home.'' There it was completely ''blown away'' to nothing by Yahweh. In spite of the echo of v. 8a, הבית (''the home'' or ''house'') should not be related to the temple (F. Peter's view); for the temple does not yet exist. Here נפח ב does not mean the animating breath, as in Gen. 2:7; Ezek. 37:9. Nor does it mean destruction through magic (J. Wellhausen), let alone a vulgarly mocking "I didn't give a hoot" (F. Peter: "Ich pfiff darauf"). What the speaker has in mind is rather a simple blowing away (cf. Ps. 1:4b; 35:5; Job 21:18; Isa. 17:13) or the annihilating blazing up of the embers of Yahweh's wrath (Isa. 54:16; Ezek. 22:20f.). At all events, the aim of the infinitive absolute and perfect forms of 9a is to gather together the fulfillment of the futility curses, so as to set the present desolate situation in *the context of a new argument.*

"Why this?" asks Yahweh. And he himself replies: "Because my house is a heap of ruins, while every one of you is running for his own house." What was loosely strung together in discussion style in vv. 4-6, in questions, admonitions and curse-fulfillment sayings, is now moved into a strict, justificatory context, in the framework of a question-answer structure. In the three-term form we have here, (1) the desolate situation is described; then (2) a question is asked about the reason; and finally (3) the answer is provided. This is a form frequently found in the framework of the Deuteronomic history's "didactic interpretation of history," as well as in the corresponding Jeremiah traditions (cf. J. W. Whedbee, "Question-Answer Scheme," *Fests. LaSor* [1978]; B. O. Long, *JBL* 90 [1971]; also L. Perlitt, *Bundestheologie im Alten Testament,* WMANT 36 [1969] 24 et passim). As (1) desolate situation the visitation of Israel's land and the city of Jerusalem can be described; in (2) the nations ask the reason; and in (3) the answer is given: they have abandoned the covenant with Yahweh and followed other gods (e.g., Deut. 29:22-28; Jer. 22:8f.). The destruction of the temple as example of desolation is found in this form only in 1 Kings 9:7-9 (2 Chron. 7:21-23). We occasionally find Yahweh's "I" (Jer. 5:18f.; 16:10-13). In Hag. 1:9 Yahweh utters both question and answer. In this form (desolation—question—answer) the desolation summed up in v. 9a is followed by Yahweh's own "Why?" and is then convincingly traced back to the people's neglect—their failure to build the temple (9b). Again Haggai shows himself to be a prophet who takes over quite rare forms of discourse in an independent way, and reshapes them. In not a single one of the comparable texts is unwillingness to build the temple given as reason for a situation of economic necessity.

Here in 9bβ,γ Haggai (similarly to v. 4) contrasts ביתי ("my house") (i.e., Yahweh's house) with ביתו "his house"—the people's own houses (cf. textual note **9c**). The concern for "his house" differs completely from the concern for "my house." The accusation is embedded in the address in 9bγ: "Each of you runs for his own house." The reproach resembles the question in v. 4. Does this sentence lend important support to the suggestion that 9(-11) is directed to quite a different group of listeners from 4(-8)? Cf. O. H. Steck, *ZAW* 83 (1971) 370. Can one say that the people "who run after their own houses" must have been homecomers from the gola who had "as yet no house," whereas it must have been the old Judaeans who "were already living in roofed-in houses"? Does not 9aβ presuppose that the people addressed here also already have their houses, into which they bring the little that they have (cf. J. W. Whedbee, op. cit., and p. 46 above)? "Each running for his own house" is a caricature which does not have to apply merely to the search for a house of one's own, or perhaps to "the reacquiring of house property owned before the exile'' (O. H. Steck, 373). It can also have meant the equipping and arrangement of the said house, outside and in. Whichever may be meant, the prophet is lamenting the false zeal which has neither time nor strength nor inclination left over for Yahweh's house. This guilt (9bβ,γ) is the reason (יַעַן, "because," 9bα,β) for the disappointment and the resulting hardship (9a).

[1:10]   But the argument goes further. A new "therefore" (עַל־כֵּן, v. 10) provides a fresh answer to the question about the consequence of guilt. Now it is no longer the human experience of hardship that is described (as in 9a; cf. 6), but its essential natural cause: the heavens have kept back all their moisture, so that the earth fails to bring forth any of its fruits. (Here too the speaker is probably drawing on curse traditions; cf. Lev. 26:20; Deut. 11:17.)

[1:11]   The main catchword for these facts follows only in v. 11: "drought" (חֹרֶב). Yet v. 11 does not merely repeat v. 10 in other words. It takes the final step that closes the chain of argument, bringing it to its goal by now making Yahweh's own "I" the subject. *Yahweh* has called forth the drought. Thus Haggai leads the people with whom he is disputing from their guilt as regards Yahweh's house (4:9b) by way of the hardships they are daily experiencing and the natural cause of these hardships (i.e., the drought, v. 10) to the originator of the drought, Yahweh (v. 11). As the Lord of creation and the judge of his people, Yahweh comes before those who have slighted his house. Haggai has repeatedly demanded that the people think about their ways, and "how they have fared" (5b, 7b). Here Yahweh himself demonstrates the connection. In vv. 9-11 a strong ring of argumentation is clinched with the help of the causal particles עַל־כֵּן—יַעַן—יַעַן מַה.

   The final transition (from 9b-10 to 11) is made by way of the imperfect consecutive וָאֶקְרָא ("and I summoned"). In the classic prophetic judgment speech, disaster resulting from guilt is also announced in Yahweh's own name ("I"). Here this form has been altered, in that the future threat has been changed into an account of the implementation of the word of judgment—an implementation that has already taken place: cf. W. A. M. Beuken, *Studien* (1967) 188; O. H. Steck, *ZAW* 83 (1971) 371: "The saying is put together out of genre elements belonging to the prophetic judgment speech, but the genre form has been altered, since it is not the judgment now announced that is justified, but an already existing situation which is interpreted and justified as a judgment that has already come to pass." Cf. also ibid., 369, n. 43. On the use of לָכֵן—יַעַן in the prophetic judgment speech cf. Amos 5:11, 16f. and H. W. Wolff, BK XIV/2, 273f. (Eng., *Joel and Amos* [1985³], 247ff.); also H. W. Wolff, "Die Begründungen der prophetischen Heils- und Unheilssprüche," *ZAW* 52 (1934) 2ff. = *Gesammelte Studien,* Theologische Bücherei 22 (1973²) 10ff. Because the people are showing their contempt for Yahweh's house, Yahweh has called forth the drought. The implemented word of judgment places listeners before their Lord, who is judging them now, in the present.

It is not rare for קרא ("call," "summon") to be used by Yahweh in the prophecy of judgment for the calling forth (employing, summoning up) of powers and forces as the instruments of Yahweh's judgment. Cf. Amos 7:4 (and the comment in H. W. Wolff, BK XIV/2, 344f. [Eng., *Joel and Amos,* 298f.]); Isa. 13:3; Jer. 25:29; Ezek. 38:21. When חֹרֶב ("drought") is called in as Yahweh's instrument, the echo of חָרֵב ("devastation") in 4b, 9b is certainly not fortuitous. חֹרֶב corresponds to חָרֵב, since the devastation—i.e., the heap of rubble which the neglectful people have permitted to lie untouched—evoked the drought. The desert waste of the ruins is both the prototype of, and the prolog to, a dry land. At considerable length, all the things are listed which are affected by the drought: the land as a whole (הארץ), and especially the hilly part of it (ההרים "the hills") by which Jerusalem is surrounded, with its plowed fields, vineyards, and olive groves. The trio "corn—wine—oil" can be found in Hosea (2:8, 22) and often in Deuteronomy (7:13; 11:14; 12:17; 14:23; 18:4; 28:51), in Jer. (31:12) and then again in the Chronicler (2 Chron. 31:5; 32:28; Neh. 5:11; 10:39; 13:5, 12). With an urge for completeness, "whatever the land brings forth" generally follows, and finally "men and cattle." (On the progression "Yahweh—heaven—earth—corn—wine—oil—human beings" cf. Hos. 2:21f. and H. W. Wolff, BK XIV/1, 65f. [Eng., *Hosea,* 1986[4], 49ff.). It will hardly be by chance that "all the laborious work of human hands" is mentioned at the end. Perhaps this is a remembrance of the futility curses on human activities (6:9a). Everything that men and women do is at the mercy of the drought.

No threat rounds off the scene-sketch. Only the exhortation and promise in v. 8 have any reference to the future. Otherwise, right to the end, all the sayings are dominated by reflections about the ways that have brought about the distresses of the present. Above all, the sayings teach that Yahweh has to be reckoned with as Lord.

On 1:12a see pp. 50-52 below.

[1:12b] The prophet's words in vv. 4-11 are followed by an account of their effect (vv. 12-14). This is not a unity. In 12a and 14 we can detect the language of the Haggai chronicler. He provides the framework for a brief, evidently older text (12b-13) which we must assume to be the continuation of the scene-sketch (see p. 34 above). Unlike 1:1, this presupposes only "the people" as Haggai's listeners; it is therefore in accordance with 1:2b and the substance of vv. 4-11 (see p. 40 above). As echo of the prophetic word, the prophet's disciple testifies merely that the people "had fear before Yahweh." Here the brief phrase ירא מפני יהוה sums up the people's acknowledgment of their guilt, and their obedience towards the prophetic exhortation. They recognize Yahweh himself in Haggai's word, just as the sayings in 8b-11 confront them with Yahweh's own "I."

[1:13] At the end of the scene the reporter has an assurance to add to the acknowledgment of guilt and the declaration of obedience. But here he does not call Haggai "the prophet," as the Haggai chronicler makes a practice of doing (1:1, 3, 12a; 2:1, 10); he describes him as a יהוה מלאך. The word "messenger" is seldom applied to prophets, though we find it in 2 Chron. 36:15f.; Isa. 44:26; cf. also the proper name "Malachi," Mal. 1:1. Derived from the root לאך = "send," "delegate" (cf. KBL[3]), the word designates the prophet as ambassador, as Yahweh's messenger; cf. K. Elliger, *Deuterojesaja*, BK XI/1 (1978) 470 on Isa. 44:26. Haggai can only be properly understood as a person appointed by Yahweh: this fact is repeatedly stressed by the appended phrase במלאכות יהוה: the promise of support which he proclaims as "saying of Yahweh" is given under "Yahweh's commission to his messenger." (And here Yahweh's name appears for the third time in v. 13.) On the assurance of support, cf. H. D. Preuss, " ' ... Ich will mit dir sein!' " *ZAW* 80 (1968) 139-173 (141ff.); D. Vetter, "עִם-mit," *THAT* II, 325-328. Generally the assurance "I am with (beside) thee (you)" appears with the preposition עִם ("with") and a singular suffix ("thee"). The form used here, with אֵת ("beside") and a plural suffix אני אתכם ("I am beside you") is otherwise found only in Jer. 42:11[1] and Hag. 2:4b (see p. 79 below). As the formula is used, it is hardly possible to detect any difference of meaning between אֵת ("beside") and עִם ("with"). אֵת may perhaps point rather to spatial nearness, עִם rather to accompaniment and fellowship; cf. W. Gesenius and F. Buhl, *Hebräisches und aramäisches Handwörterbuch zum AT* (1921[17]). Haggai's saying ought then to be translated "I am at your side," "I am beside you" (Isa. 30:8; 43:5;[2] Exod. 33:21). The assurance of support belongs to the "priestly salvation oracle" which we find taken up particularly frequently in Deutero-Isaiah; cf. Isa. 41:10; 43:2, 5; Jer. 30:10f.; see on this J. Begrich, "Das priesterliche Heilsorakel," *ZAW* 52 (1934) 81-92 (esp. 82f.) = his *Gesammelte Studien*, TB 21 (1964) 217-231 (esp. 219f.). In our Haggai saying the promise of support is a response to the "fear of Yahweh" that has been expressed (v. 12b). Once the people have recognized their failings and their mistaken zeal (vv. 4, 9), they will already be permitted a foretaste of Yahweh's presence (on 8b see pp. 45f. above).

On 1:14 see pp. 52f. below.

[1:12a]   At the close of the prophetic scene-sketch (12b-13), the Haggai chronicler offers a detailed interpretation (12a, 14). First of all he expounds the way in which "fear of Yahweh" (12b) is to be understood. It manifests itself, or comes about, in a "listening to the voice of Yahweh and to the words of Haggai the prophet," though שמע ב ("listen to") does not mean solely that the ears are called into service. "Listening" is also the work of the heart; i.e., it means perception, will, and hence obedience; cf. A. K. Fenz, *Auf Jahwes Stimme hören* (1964) 38f., 44-50, 65. The phrase שמע בקול יהוה אלהים "listen to the voice of Yahweh Elohim"—in which יהוה ("Yahweh") can be replaced by a suffix to קול

---

[1] RSV translates: "with" (trans.).
[2] RSV translates: "with" (trans.).

("voice") and אלהים ("Elohim") can have a suffix linking it with the listeners: "your" God—is found about 70 times in the Old Testament, 85% of these instances occurring in Deuteronomy (e.g., 8:20; 13:18; 15:5), in the Deuteronomic sections of the book of Jeremiah (e.g., 3:25; 7:28; 26:13) and of the Deuteronomic history (e.g., Josh. 24:24; 1 Sam. 12:15; 2 Kings 18:12); cf. also W. Thiel, *Die deuteronomistische Redaktion von Jeremia 1-25,* WMANT 41 (1973) 86. Whereas the scene-sketch stresses that it is Yahweh whom the people encounter in his ambassador Haggai (13a, see pp. 49f. above), parallel phraseology now explains that by listening to the words of Haggai the prophet, his hearers have listened to Yahweh's voice; and that in the words of Haggai the prophet, the voice of Yahweh was obeyed. The parallelism corresponds to the sending of Haggai by Yahweh, just as then the כאשר clause ("just as") justifies the prophet's authority as being grounded on Yahweh's commission and on the identity between his proclamation of Yahweh's word and Yahweh's own will; 12a takes up in its own words what the writer found in his copy in 13a. On the connection of meaning between (מלאך) לאך and שלח שלח cf. R. Ficker, "מלאך—Bote," *THAT* I, 900f., 903. שלח ("send") is used for the sending of a prophet incomparably more often than מלאך (see p. 50 above) and remains characteristic of prophecy (Isa. 6:8; Jer. 1:7; Ezek. 2:3; Zech. 4:9; Mal. 3:1, ;4:25). The word corresponds to the messenger formula (כה) אמר יהוה ("[thus] says Yahweh"), which is so frequent in Haggai: 1:2, 5, 7f.; 2:6f., 9, 11; cf. the divine oracle formula נאם יהוה ("saying of Yahweh") in 1:9, 13; 2:4a,β, 8, 9, 14, 17, 23aα,β, bβ and the excursus on p. 100 below.

A curious point is connected with the person whom the Haggai chronicler tells us listened to the prophet's oracle. That Zerubbabel is named first as listener corresponds to his position as addressee of the confronting event of God's word in 1:1. But why is the official designation "governor of Judah" lacking, although it is never missing either in 1:1 or in 1:14; 2:2; or 2:21? That it should not appear in the direct address in 2:4 and 2:23 is more understandable, although in 2:4 Joshua is addressed with his official title, directly after the untitled Zerubbabel. (The name of Zerubbabel's father, Shealtiel, is missing only in 2:4 and 21.) The name of Joshua's father and his office never fail once to be mentioned. Zerubbabel would seem to be the better known figure, and for Haggai the more important of the two. He is always mentioned first (cf. also Ezra 2:2; 3:8; 4:2; 5:2; Zech. 4:6, 7, 9, 10; Sir. 49:11) and must have played the leading part in the building of the temple, at least in the initial stages (Zech. 4:9). The title "governor of Judah" may perhaps have been too much of a reminder that he was acting under Persian authority. For Haggai and his chronicler, Zerubbabel is in the ultimate resort "Yahweh's servant" (2:23). It is also through Yahweh's word alone that he sees himself strengthened in 2:4, and it is through that word that he is already here in 1:12a subdued to obedience. On the other hand there was no tension between Joshua's position as high priest and the building of the temple.

A striking feature about the list of the prophet's listeners is the mention of "the whole remnant of the people." שארית ("remnant") is a term which is applied to the exiles as bearers of the promise. It becomes the title to salvation for the people who survived. It is widely used in exilic prophecy (cf. Isa. 46:3; Jer. 23:3; Mic. 2:12; 4:7; Zeph. 3:13 and frequently; also H. W. Wolff, *Micha,* BK XIV/4 [1982] 95). The term is applied first of all to the people "who had escaped from the sword" at the deportations of 597 and 587 (2 Kings 19:31; Ezra 9:14; 2 Chron. 36:20) and later to homecomers from the gola (Neh. 7:71; cf. Mic. 7:18; Jer. 44:28; Zech. 8:6, 11f.). In the Deuteronomic book of Jeremiah, chaps. 42-44, "the remnant of Judah" is the invariable description of the people who had been driven apart into neighboring states and then returned home again under Gedaliah. It was also applied to the people who had emigrated to Egypt; cf. Jer. 43:5; 40:11, 15; 42:2, 15, 19; 44;12, 14, 28. It is significant that the Haggai chronicler does not talk about "the remnant of Judah" like those chapters from the late exilic period (cf. W. Thiel, *Die deuteronomistische Redaktion von Jeremia 26–45,* 65, 78f.). He talks about "the whole remnant of the people." Haggai's "remnant of the people" must be distinguished from the original Judaeans who had never been deported (cf. K. Galling, *Studien* [1964] 75, 136 and E. Janssen, *Juda in der Exilszeit,* FRLANT 69 [1956] 119 n. 3). שארית cannot be considered another name for the postexilic population of Jerusalem and Judah, because in Ezra 3:8; 4:1; 6:16 it is explicitly the sons from the gola who are attested as being the builders of the new temple. Haggai and the author of the scene-sketches have not hitherto noticeably distinguished between the old Judaeans and the homecomers (cf. 1:2 and 12b, 13a). Why is "the whole remnant of the people" now added to the obedient hearers Zerubbabel and Joshua? The phrase refers to that section of the people who were descended from prominent circles in Jerusalem, whereas the poorer ones had never been deported (cf. 2 Kings 25:11f.). It was on these groups that Zerubabbel and Joshua, themselves homecomers, had the strongest influence, in the light of their common history as bearers of the promise and as returned exiles (cf. p. 96 below). These are the people who will most readily have had an ear for the new prophetic word, since they were the group who were mentally more alert and economically more vigorous and who, moreover, were not without financial resources, as the list of donations shows; cf. Neh. 7:70-72 and K. Galling, *Studien,* 56f., 89f., 101-103. So under the authoritative leadership of the governor and the high priest, they soon turned from listening to doing.

On 1:12b, 13 see pp. 49-50 above.

[1:14] But, since the scene-sketch ended in v. 13 with the assurance of Yahweh's support, the chronicler does not allow acts to follow immediately on hearing: for him, Yahweh's special intervention still has to come first. "Yahweh roused the spirit of Zerubbabel ... and of Joshua ... and of the whole remnant of the people." עור *hiphil* describes the waking of the person who is asleep or drowsy (Zech. 4:1; Isa. 50:4), the activating of the inert, the spurring on of the indolent (Isa. 41:2, 25; 45:13). In this context רוח means a person's willpower (cf. H. W. Wolff, *Anthropologie des Alten Testaments,* 65-67 [Eng. *Anthropology of the Old Testament,* 1974, 37-39]). Thus we should probably distinguish the phrase העיר את רוח from the gift of Yahweh's spirit to human beings (Ezek. 11:19; 36:26f.; Joel 2:28f.

[שׁפּר/נתן את־רוח [יהוה]); cf. Zech. 4:6; Hag. 2:5aβ and pp. 79f. below. By moving the human will to activity, Yahweh brings hearers to act. An "arousal" of this kind is experienced, not merely by members of God's people (cf. Jer. 51:11; 1 Chron. 5:26; 2 Chron. 21:16) but also by the Persian Cyrus, for example (Isa. 41:2, 25; 45:13). In the phrase העיר את־רוח ("stir up the spirit"), Yahweh's activating power always serves his rule over history, not an individual "religious revival" (H. Bardtke, *Erweckungsgedanke* [1958] 16-19). This is true especially of the "stirring up of the spirit of Cyrus" (2 Chron. 36:22ff.; Ezra 1:1ff.), the purpose of which was to bring home the exiles and to build the temple. Thus "stirring up the spirit" does not merely help individuals to strength of will; the whole community can experience it. This is also the premise of Ezra 1:5. In the same way here, not only Zerubbabel and Joshua are affected but "the whole remnant of the people"—i.e., the whole community of returned exiles. Consequently—and this is in accordance with the Cyrus texts—the turning point of history, which will find its fulfillment after the return of still other groups from exile, has come closer; now its fulfillment may be expected, with the building of the temple. It is Yahweh himself who has aroused the necessary will power (14a).

It is only now (14b) that the listeners who have been "aroused" become the subject of the account: "they came and took up the work." ויבאו, "and they came," shows the movement which followed forthwith (see textual note **2a-a**). People gathered together for consultation in the temple ruins, for the very first, preparatory work, perhaps before starting out into the hills to fetch wood, in accordance with Haggai's exhortation in v. 8a. The phrase עשׂה מלאכה, "take up work," comprises the whole work of rebuilding; ויעשׂוּ, imperfect consecutive, should here be understood inchoatively—as representing the beginning of the action. מלאכה is to be found particularly frequently in Exodus 35f. and in the Chronicler's history for all kinds of work (carried out at someone's commission) and particularly for especially skilled work on the sanctuary (cf. J. Milgrom and D. P. Wright, "מלאכה," *ThWAT* IV, 906). Ezra 3:8 and 6:22 formulate "work on Yahweh's house" very similarly (מלאכה בית יהוה). Ezra 2:69; Neh. 7:70 mention a אוצר המלאכה, a "treasury of the work"—probably a "building fund" filled up by donations, out of which wages and the cost of the necessary materials could be paid (Ezra 3:7; Neh. 7:71; cf. K. Galling, *Studien* [1964] 103). The fact that in all this the object was "the house of Yahweh of hosts, their God" is stressed at the close of the Haggai chronicler's first account of the confronting event of the word.

It is difficult to link v. 15a with v. 14, since what is described are not events that could be pinpointed to any single day, but a more sustained process spread over three and a half weeks (cf. 1:1, 12a, 14a with 15a)—unless, indeed, we were to relate 1:15a only to 1:14b, as is probably intended by the final redaction. See pp. 34f. above and 59f. below.

Purpose and Thrust

Haggai's purpose in the disputation with his people is unequivocal: "Build Yahweh's house!" (8a). Nothing could be more terse or more specific: "Off to the hills to fetch wood!'' Here everyone can immediately lend a hand (see p. 45 above). The goal is clear.

But there is violent opposition. People are running busily for their own houses (4, 9b). They are eagerly engaged in making a living for themselves (6, 9a). There is no time left for building the temple (2b, 4a). Is there any way of overcoming the no to the prophetic call?

Haggai doesn't threaten. Haggai doesn't accuse. Haggai argues. ''Consider how you have fared!'' (5b, 7b; see p. 43 above). Set the way you have behaved over against what has happened to you! The prophet and his people share a common starting point: their present, grim experience of hard times. But the conclusions they draw are different. The people say: ''Because the times are hard there is no time for the temple'' (2b, 9a). Haggai counters: ''It is because you have no time for the temple that the times are hard'' (9b). The prophet reverses cause and effect, and thereby strips bare the truth. And he can add the argument that clinches it all: the hard times can be traced back to Yahweh's word (9b-11).

Is this Haggai not *too* ''minor'' a prophet? Is his motivation not centered on material prosperity alone? Is he not a prisoner of the notion of retaliation (cf. F. Hesse, ''Haggai,'' *Verbannung und Heimkehr: Fests. W. Rudolph* [1961] 109-134)? He intervenes simply and solely in order to bring about the building of the temple. Does this not manifest overt indifference to ethical and spiritual goals (cf. F. James, *JBL* 53 [1934] 235; B. S. Childs, *Introduction to the Old Testament as Scripture* [1979] 466f.)? We need only compare Amos and Isaiah, or even Zech 1:6; 7:5ff.; 8:14ff.!

Yet does he not display a certain greatness of his own? Cf. G. von Rad, *Theologie des Alten Testaments* [1962^4] II, 291f. (Eng. *Old Testament Theology* [1975^2], II, 282). He associates the tiniest beginnings of a rebuilding (''Fetch wood!'' 8a) with the mighty assurance of his God: ''I will show myself in my glory'' (8b; see p. 46 above). Thus in the midst of wretchedly poor conditions, he sees the glint of something completely new, something unexpected and undeserved. He links the first tiny steps with the great experience of God's presence. And yet he remains astonishingly down-to-earth.

His reporter has preserved the fact that in his own way Haggai brought his people to ''fear God,'' and that he assured them of his God's support (12b-13; see pp. 49f. above). The fact that he brought about the beginning of the temple's reconstruction is not reported.

That fact is brought out in the great editorial process in which the prophetic scene-sketches (1:4-11, 12b-13) were absorbed as main element into the documentary chronicle recording the beginnings of the temple's rebuilding (1-3, 12a, 14; see pp. 50f. above). If the aim of the scene-sketches was merely to show how the people were brought to fear God, the Haggai chronicler now contributes the precise facts about the effect of Haggai's sayings. He defines the goal of his account in 14b: ''They took up the work on the house of Yahweh.'' And he answers the questions: Who? When? Why? How?

Who? The governor Zerubbabel is always mentioned first of all

(1:1, 12a, 14; see p. 51 above), and after him Joshua, for whose ministry the temple is indispensable. The section of the people mentioned is "all the remnant of the people"—that is to say, the returned exiles, whom Haggai and his witness had not specially mentioned (see p. 40 above).

When? The date—the first day of the sixth month in the second year of Darius's reign (= August 29, 520)—documents the new era which Haggai's initiative represented in the life of the postexilic community: the era of the first temple and its destruction is drawing to an end. A new era—the era of the second temple—is beginning with the datable event of a confronting divine word.

Why was the rebuilding taken in hand? Three times the Haggai chronicler stresses Yahweh's act in "rousing the spirit" (14a): the willpower of Zerubbabel, the willpower of Joshua, and the willpower of the whole community of returned exiles was roused by Israel's God—roused by him alone, but by him roused irresistibly. Without the exiled people whom Yahweh led home—the people who had experienced the divine judgment in its harshest form but who had been carried through and saved—the rebuilding would probably never have taken place.

But how it happened can in the chronicler's view be clearly traced back to the prophet Haggai. That is why he begins his documentation with the introduction of the prophetic event of the word (vv. 1-3). That is why he takes over the record of Haggai's sayings (4-11, 2b, 13b). That is why he stresses that the people who were prepared to undertake the rebuilding had recognized in Haggai's words the voice of Yahweh (12a).

With this documentation, the community of the new temple is to remember that its restored house of God means that a particular divine word, communicated through the prophet, has been fulfilled, in spite of the people's recalcitrance (2b, 9b). Even a "minor" prophet can bring about great things. And for 500 years this "great thing" documented the hope for God's ultimate dwelling among men and women.

Second Scene:
The Turn to Blessing

Literature

E. Sellin, *Studien zur Entstehungsgeschichte der jüdischen Gemeinde* II (1901). J. W. Rothstein, *Juden und Samaritaner*, BWAT 3 (1908) 53-73. A. Fernández, "El Profeta Ageo 2,15-18 y la fundación del segundo templo," *Bibl* 2 (1921) 206-215. A. Gelston, "The Foundations of the Second Temple," *VT* 16 (1966) 232-235. K. Koch, "Haggais unreines Volk," *ZAW* 79 (1967) 52-66. W. H. Schmidt, "יסד—gründen," *THAT* I (1971) 736f. R. Mosis, "יסד," *ThWAT* III (1982) 668-682 (676f., 680f.). D. J. Clark, "Problems in Haggai 2.15-19," *The Bible Translator* 34 (1983) 432-439.

Text

1:15a On the twenty-fourth day of the month [in the sixth][a] . . .

2:15 [But now:][a]
      just direct your attention
         from this day onward!
      Before you[b] placed stone to stone
         on Yahweh's temple:

16   [a]how did you fare?[a]
     When one came[b] to the heap of corn
        that ought to amount to twenty (measures),
           there were (only) ten.
     When one came[b] to the winepress [winevat][c]
        to draw fifty (measures),
           there were (only) twenty.

17   [a] [I smote you with blight and mildew,
     with hail all the work of your hands.
     Yet there was no [b]return among you[b] to me—saying of Yahweh].[a]

57

18 Just direct your attention
    from this day onward!
    ^a[from the twenty-fourth day of the ninth (month),
    that is^b from the day^c when Yahweh's temple was restored.
    ^dDirect your attention to it!^d]^a

19 Certainly,^a the seed is still in the corn-pit,
    still^a ^b[the vine, the fig-tree and the pomegranate]^b
    the olive tree yields nothing.
    But^c from this day on I will bless.

1:15a-a בַּשִּׁשִּׁי ("in the sixth") instead of הַשִּׁשִּׁי ("the sixth") (cf. 1:1a) or לַשִּׁשִּׁי ("of the sixth") (cf. 2:1a, 10a, 18b, 20) shows that the word has been added subsequently (W. Nowack). The glossator probably wished to avoid confusion with the 24th day in the ninth month (2:10, 18b, 20). Cf. E. Sellin, KAT XII, 459.

2:15a When 1:15a was cut off from the passage now appearing in 2:15ff., words were lost, and at the beginning of 2:15 וְעַתָּה ("but now") was subsequently added, in order—after the relocation of the original text to (now) 2:15-19—to relate that text emphatically to the "now" of the 24th day of the 9th month (= December 18). Cf. 18bα with 2:10 and pp. 62f. below. F. Horst's proposal is worthy of mention: he suggests inserting before the cry the words: הָיָה דְבַר־יהוה בְּיַד חַגַּי הַנָּבִיא אֶל־זְרֻבָּבֶל בֶּן־שְׁאַלְתִּיאֵל פַּחַת יְהוּדָה וְאֶל־יְהוֹשֻׁעַ בֶּן־יְהוֹצָדָק הַכֹּהֵן הַגָּדוֹל וְאֶל־כֹּל שְׁאֵרִית הָעָם לֵאמֹר ("the word of Yahweh went out through Haggai the prophet to Zerubbabel, son of Shaltiel, governor of Judah, and to Joshua, son of Jehozadak, the high priest, and to all the remnant of the people"). His reason is that the Haggai chronicler hardly ever introduces a dated report without an introduction of this kind; cf. 1:1; 2:1f., 10, 20. J. W. Rothstein (*Juden*, 64) wished to supplement the saying in accordance with 1:5a. But see p. 60 below. In this case we should have to suppose that the Haggai chronicler left the date in 1:15a attached to 1:14b in order that he might move the original passage now 2:15-19 to its present position after 2:14. For his reasons see pp. 67f. below.

15b The subject (2nd person plural) of the infinitive absolute is determined by the context; see textual note **1:9a-a** above.

16a-a MT seems incomprehensible (M. Buber interprets: *ehe sie da waren*, "before they were there"). Gk τίνες ἦτε ("as what were you?") will have read מַה־הֱיִיתֶם (or מִי), "how were you? how did you stand? (K. Marti). The 2nd person plural form of address in Gk fits the context better than the 3rd person plural suffix in MT.

16b Perhaps בֹּא ("come") should be read as an infinitive absolute. This is Marti's view, following 1:9.

16c The word פוּרָה is otherwise found only in Isa. 63:3, where RSV translates it "wine press." It cannot be viewed as a later interpretative gloss, however, for יקב is a much more common word for winepress and would have required no explanation. Is פוּרָה intended to serve here as a (subsequently added) unit of measure? Cf. W. Rudolph 45f., textual note to 2:16f. K. Galling, "Wein und Weinbereitung," *BRL*² 362, interprets פוּרָה as a word signifying the whole area involved in the wine making, which consisted of the treading floor (גַּת) and the vat (יקב) in which the wine was collected.

17a-a The whole verse explains and expands v. 16. Since the beginning especially is highly reminiscent of Amos 4:9, it must be viewed as a gloss. Cf. textual notes 2:14**a-a** and **c**; also p. 62 below.

17b-b 17b is hardly comprehensible as it stands. M. Buber translates MT *aber zu mir hin* *gabs nichts bei euch* (literally "but in you there was nothing that turned to me"). Gk: οὐκ ἐπεστρέψατε πρὸς με ("you did not return to me") and Vg *et non fuit in vobis qui reverteretur ad me* ("and there was no one among you who returned to me") suggests that after ואין only שוב has disappeared and that instead of אֶתְכֶם we should vocalize אַתְכֶם. Another proposal adheres less closely to the transmitted MT. According to this view, we should read וְלֹא שַׁבְתֶּם אֵלַי ("but you did not return to me") as a free adaptation of the refrain in Amos 4:6-11). E. Sellin changes only a single consonant (and the vocalization of a single word) to read "I was not with you" (וְאֵין אַתְכֶם אָנִי); cf. 1:13b; 2:4b.

18a-a 18b offers a series of subsequent interpretations about the day of the change to blessing (18a) which Haggai announces. J. W. Rothstein (p. 58) already pointed this out. See p. 65 below.

18b ל introduces more precise explanations, in the sense of "namely" (cf. Jer. 1:18; 2 Chron. 28:15 and KBL[3] 485a, no. 22). Gk translates merely καὶ ἀπό ("and from") = וּמִן.

18c The composite preposition merely states the terminus a quo (W. A. M. Beuken, 209).

18d-d The repetition of 18aα became necessary at this point because the extensive amplifications had removed the demand too far from its actual object (19a).

19a Instead of וְעַד "and until" in 19aβ, וְעֹד ("still") should be read, parallel to 19aα and following Gk (εἰ ἔτι). The adverb הַ, which is usually an interrogative particle, can occasionally have an exclamatory meaning: "True!" (restrictive); cf. Joüon, *Gr* §161b and W. A. M. Beuken, 212f.

19b-b נשׂא ("bears") at the end of the sentence presupposes a singular subject. The three fruit trees mentioned before the olive have no doubt been added later, so as to make clear the full extent of the failed harvest, and in order to proclaim the wealth of the blessing.

19c The asyndetic transition to the final sentence (i.e., without the copulative ו) emphasizes the contrast; cf. BrSynt §134a,e.

Form

To what is the date in 1:15a related? It is impossible to link it with 1:15b, since this half-verse cannot be detached from 2:1, where it corresponds to the order of the date in 1:1 (year—month—day). It is certainly quite feasible to relate 1:15a to 1:14b as far as its content goes, since there is no reason why work on the temple should not have been taken up 3½ weeks after Haggai's great polemic on the first day of the sixth month (1:1 = August 29; see p. 53 above). Nonetheless, stylistically speaking this seems unlikely. For elsewhere the Haggai chronicler always puts the date, which is part of his general practice, at *the beginning* of the prophetic speeches (see p. 31f.). The dates do not always have to be set out as fully as they are in 1:1; 1:15b—2:2; and 2:10, however, where they introduce the confronting event of God's word. If he is introducing a new section that is closely connected, in time or content, with what has gone before (as in 2:20) he can restrict himself to a statement of the day, as here in 1:15a.

But what has happened to the prophetic sayings belonging to 1:15a? Ever since E. Sellin (*Studien* [1901]), J. W. Rothstein, (*Juden und Samaritaner* [1908]) and H. G. Mitchell (*Haggai*, ICC [1912]), scholars have been convinced that they were to be found in 2:15-19. Reasons of form and content suggest that the substantial elements of 2:15-19 were originally placed after 1:15a and before 1:15b—2:9, and that the present position of the passage between 2:10-14 and 2:20-23 was the result of secondary, or later, intervention. The distinction "clean—unclean" in the didactic discussion with the priests, and the designation of "this people" as "unclean" (2:10-14) finds no echo in 2:15-19. (The stylistically conforming repetition in 17aβ of the phrase כל־מעשׂה ידיהם ["all the work of their hands"] from 2:14aβ, as well as the repetition of the dating of 2:10 in 2:18bα, are obviously later additions; see p. 62 below.) Instruction and judgment: that is the character of 2:(10-)14. It is in marked contrast to the elements that go to the making of 2:15-19— utterances in a lively dialog style, in the form of direct address, with exhortations and questions, ultimately issuing in a promise. These utterances are far more reminiscent of the discussion style of the first scene-sketch in 1:4-11. (On the characteristics of the scene-sketch, including this passage, see pp. 21, 33f. above and W. A. M. Beuken, *Studien* [1967] 214.) The appeal to consider in 2:15 and 18a is reminiscent of the admonition to reflection in 1:5b, 7b, down to the very wording.

The content accords with the stylistic closeness to the first disputation. The call to begin building the temple (1:8) has now been followed by the day when, for the first time, "stone was placed to stone" (2:15). Verses 1:14b and 1:15a link the first two scenes together, both in time and content. The land is still burdened by the extremity of drought (cf. 2:16, 19a with 1:6, 9-11). But in place of the curse on the neglectful people (1:6, 9; see p. 44 above), the beginning of the building is accompanied by the assurance of blessing (2:15, 19b). So 1:15a, together with the substance of 2:15-19, as a saying uttered at the start of the building work on the 24th day of the 6th month = September 21, 520, fits best in time and content, as well as stylistically, immediately after 1:1-14 (on the 1st day of the 6th month = August 29, 520) and before 1:15b—2:9; for here—on the 21st day of the 7th month = October 17, 520—the presumption is that the first signs of weariness over the building were making themselves felt (2:3f.). The present assignment of 2:15-19 to the 24th day of the 9th month (= December 18, 520; see 2:10 and 18b) is much too remote (by almost four months) from Haggai's first exhortation on the 1st day of the 6th month (= August 29, 520). The report in 1:12a, 14 contradicts all too clearly the date given, even if we were to assume with K. Galling (*Studien*, 136) that the preliminary clearance work required a considerable time. The reasons for linking 1:15a with the substance of 2:15-19 would appear to be more cogent.

Setting

However, so radical an intervention in the present text on literary grounds demands an answer to the question: why has the passage been moved to its present position? What could be the purpose? O. Kaiser (*Einleitung in das Alten Testament* [1984[5]] 286) thinks that the reviser wished to prevent the final comment on the people in the little book from being an unfavorable one. I myself find E. Elliger's proposal more probable: he suspects that an editor wished to link the end of "the time of troubles" with the rejection of "the Samaritans," in accordance with 2:14.

In line with this supposition, I should like to suggest the possibility that the repositioning of the substance of 2:15-19 is connected with the working-up of the prophetic scene-sketches by the Haggai chronicler whom we met in 1:1-3, 12a, 14 (see pp. 32f. above). We saw in 1:12a, 14— and shall see again in 2:2—that according to the Haggai chronicler it was "the whole remnant of the people" returning from the gola that had obeyed the prophetic call to build the temple. The Haggai chronicler evidently finds it important to define more closely "the people" to whom Haggai himself appeals (1:2, 12b, 13; 2:4). In 2:10-14, what is under discussion is evidently a possible expansion of the group who are to cooperate in the building, an expansion designed to include in the work certain groups of the old, established inhabitants; but these are rejected as being "unclean" (2:14; cf. Ezra 4:1-5 and p. 92 below). The date when a decision was made about the people on whom the rebuilding of the temple was to depend, seems to have been an important one for the Haggai chronicler. It was only when this question had been decided that, in his view, the building of the temple could legitimately begin. So for him the 24th day of the 9th month (= December 18, 520), as stated in 2:18b, not the 24th day of the 6th month (= September 21), as given in 1:15, was "the day" when the turn to blessing came about ("from this day onward," 2:18a, 19). This means that the appeal to be attentive (2:15, 18a) must be postponed to an ending of the drought three months later. Did the rains perhaps begin particularly late in the winter of 520/19?

The shifting of 2:15-19 to its present position after 2:10-14 involved minor textual changes. It has been assumed that instead of ועתה ("but now") at the beginning of 2:15 and after 1:15a, the Haggai chronicler's usual introductory note should be added, on the lines of 1:1 and 1:15b—2:2 (see textual note to 2:15**a**). But if the Haggai chronicler himself carried out the transposition of 2:15-19 and the detachment from 1:15a, then the present ועתה ("but now") must be his as well (see p. 63 below). It prepares for the shift of date from the 24th day of the 6th month (= September 21) to the 24th day of the 9th month (= December 18); cf. 1:15a with 2:10, 18b. But 1:15a remains in its original position, though now as a date for 1:14b.

Verse 18b of chapter 2 pins down the redating more precisely. All three parts of the sentence are linked, as subsequent interpretation, with the wording of the already existing, preceding scene-sketch. מיום ("from the day") in bα takes up מן־היום הזה ("from this day onward") from aβ, as well as למן־היום in bβ ("that is from the day"), where ל-*explicativum* (see textual note **18b**) could point to a second stage in the editorial process, in which the date is further elucidated by the event that takes place on that day. The final part of the sentence takes up in terser form the call to attentiveness in 2:15 and 18a, in order—after the interpolations— to emphasize the tenor of the text once more, before v. 19. In content the first two phrases in 18b are also linked with what has already been said: the dating in bα takes up the introductory date in 2:10, the day marked by the event of the first work on the foundations, bβ being a reminiscence of the "placing stone to stone" of the earlier scene-sketch, 2:15b. Yet it must remain an open question whether 18b as a whole goes back to the editorial work of the Haggai chronicler, or is (at least in part) a later gloss. See the Introduction, §3, above.

Verse 17 must also be viewed as a later addition. It takes over precisely the first four words of Amos 4:9a, as well as the substance of 4:9b; in 2:17 αβ כֹל־ מֵעֲשֵׂה יְדֵיהֶם ("all the work of their hands") has been taken over from 2:14bα, and has merely been transposed into the form of direct address ("your hands"). The verse does not really correspond to the central message of the text, which is a demand for expectation of a revolution in the times, from disaster to salvation. Instead of that, this verse lets the gaze linger on the time of troubles that has prevailed hitherto, and in doing so fails entirely to match stylistically the statements in vv. 16 and 19a.

In 19aβ also the first four words must be viewed as a subsequently added intensification of the poor harvest that has already been described. The three interpolated trees are found in the same order in Joel 1:12. The singular נָשָׂא ("yields") of the older text points only to the olive tree. The fact that vines, fig trees, and pomegranates bear no fruit is a later, somber intensification of the time of distress. What has been hitherto is more vividly present than the promised future. The revisers were continually preoccupied with what was lacking, simply because that provided the features by which the turn of events could be recognized.

Questions about the place and time of the promise of blessing in 2:15f., 18a, and 19 have occupied scholars, as was to be expected in view of the somewhat turbulent history of the early text. The promise was probably originally proclaimed by the prophet Haggai three and one-half weeks after the oracles in 1:4-11 (according to 1:15a, on the 24th day of the 6th month = September 21, 520). It therefore accompanied the very first official beginning of work on the temple. This was the start of more than the planning and the preliminaries, for which there had been sufficient time beforehand, after (perhaps) earlier, first attempts (Ezra 4:24; 5:16) and according to 1:12-14. Otherwise the prophet would not have thrice emphasized "this day" (2:15a, 18a, 19b). Now "stone was placed to stone" (see pp. 63 below). The phrase points to the first work on the foundations. In a continuation of the message of 1:4-11 (see pp. 44f. above), Haggai, standing in the temple area, now proclaims the great reversal from the state of distress to an era of better things (2:16, 19).

This text from the 24th day of the 6th month (= September 21) was in its original wording probably noted down in the context of a scene-sketch in which the prophet appeared. The Haggai chronicler has taken it over and has assigned it to a new "Now" (וְעַתָּה 2:15aα)—namely, the day when the "unclean people" were rejected, according to 2:(10-)14; see p. 61 above and pp. 95f. below. He sees the turn to blessing as given only when this decision had been taken. The new assignment (on literary grounds) of 2:15f., 18a, 19 to 2:10-14 leads to a new dating in 2:18bα (to the 24th day of the 9th month = December 18; 2:18bα following 2:10). This day is thereby also designated as the day when work on the foundations of the temple began (2:18bβ, following 2:15b). The secondary character of these statements in 18b is unmistakable (see pp. 61f. above). Here the revision of a text according to literary and theological criteria—probably by the Haggai chronicler—

has led to the false dating of a historical event (which actually took place on the 24th day of the 6th month = September 21, 520, according to 1:15a). It is, after all, extremely improbable that work on the temple should have begun in December, in the middle of the rainy season.

Commentary

[1:15a] As we have seen (pp. 59ff. above), v. 1:15a was originally linked with 2:15, and was only subsequently assigned to 1:14b. Over against the false date in 2:18b, which assigned 2:15-19* to the 24th day of the 9th month, the note subsequently added in 1:15a, "in the sixth (month)," seemed to us correct and important (see textual note 1:15**a**). The dispute about the date determines our decision with regard to the various ideas about the beginnings of work on the temple. Our literary analysis (pp. 62f. above) showed that what was initiated on the 24th day of the 6th month (= September 21) was not merely the consultation, planning, and decrees of Zerubbabel and Joshua. It was not even the very first clearing-up work, the removal of the mountains of rubble and the acquisition of the necessary material. This was the day when work on the foundations began—that is to say, the actual labor of reconstruction.

[2:15] It is hardly conceivable that, after the impression made by Haggai's words, the whole time from the 1st to the 24th day of the 6th month (from August 29 until September 21) should have passed by without any preparatory measures having been taken. After the prophet had been "listened to," these weeks will have been marked from the very first day onwards by the "rousing" of good will and will have been occupied by the "taking up" of the preparatory work (1:12a, 14). The fact that a new date is mentioned (the 24th day of the 6th month = September 21) is only comprehensible if this date marked some outstanding occasion. That occasion is described in 2:15 as the truly decisive event: the people "placed stone to stone on Yahweh's temple." From Haggai's point of view, only the real beginning of the building work, which is described in this phrase, makes his three separate mentions of "this day" (היום הזה) in 2:15a, 18a, and 19b comprehensible.

The phrase "placed stone to stone" occurs only here in the whole of the Old Testament. What must be meant are the "great, costly stones" which already formed part of the foundation of Solomon's temple, according to 1 Kings 5:17; 7:10f. (cf. Ezra 6:4). The expression does not permit us to think of a raising of the walls in the general sense (A. S. van der Woude's view: *Haggai* [1982]). Nor does it point to the ceremonial laying of the foundation stone at the beginning of construction (F. Horst, HAT I/14 [1964³]), as if we were supposed to think of a single stone. S. Amsler (CAT XIc [1981] 30) takes up the studies of A. Petitjean (*Les oracles du Proto-Zacharie* [1969] 216-226), according to which, in Mesopotamian texts, in the reconstruction of a sanctuary that had been destroyed, a foundation stone belonging to the old sanctuary was incorporated by the king in the foundation of the new temple. But Haggai's way of expressing the matter does not suggest any similar, special liturgical act. We should rather assume with K. Galling (*Studien* [1964] 130) and T. A. Busink (*Tempel* [1980] 804), in analogy to ancient Mesopotamian building customs and on the basis of Ezra 6:3, that when a ruined temple was rebuilt, the old foundation was retained. We are nowhere told that a new foundation was laid. If it is permissible to see 2:18bβ (יסד *puʿal*, "set," "place") as interpreting 2:15b, then what is meant is the taking up of work to restore the building, the building being היכל יהוה, "Yahweh's temple." It is only in 2:15 (as in the—secondary—2:18bβ; and cf. Ezra 3:10) that Haggai uses this word for the temple. Otherwise he always speaks of "Yahweh's house": 1:2, 4b, 8, 9bβ, [14]; 2:3, 7, 9. היכל means the main room of the temple, the "assembly hall" (M. Noth, *Könige* I 1–16, BK IX/1 [1983²] on 1 Kings 6:17), between the vestibule and the Holy of Holies. With the "placing stone to stone" on a particular day, the real restoration begins. The fact that the occasion was formally celebrated is evidenced solely by Haggai's brief speech on that day (cf. now D. L. Petersen, *Haggai* [1984] 89f.).

As he does in his exhortations in 1:5b, 17b, Haggai again demands "the orientation of the heart"—that is, expectant attentiveness. The object of this attention is not now supposed to be the link between behavior and "destiny," or experience of life ("ways"; see p. 43 above), but rather the turn to a new era, which the people are to hope for with "this present day." The witnesses of the beginning of the building are supposed to observe with tense expectancy how differently life is experienced before and after this day. The adverbs of time מן־היום הזה ומעלה) and מטרם point to contrasts. In its spatial sense, מעלה means "higher" (Deut. 28:43), "above" (1 Kings 7:11), "upward" (Judges 1:36). In a temporal sense, as here, it means "further," "from now on," "henceforth," "in the future" (1 Sam. 16:13; 30:25). The word (מ)טרם on the other hand means "not yet" (Gen. 2:5), "even before" (Ps. 90:2) or "before" (Ps. 119:67). That is to say, it points back to what is past, to what has been hitherto, to what has been superseded. Haggai declares that "this present day" is the precise borderline between what has existed hitherto, which is defined as past and gone, and the future that is to be expected, which Yahweh is going to bring about. The call to expect this turn of events dominates the whole saying, as its repetition in 18a shows.

[2:16] What we find between vv. 15 and 18 is what Wellhausen called "a parenthetic preparation for the main idea by way of a necessary antithesis" (*Die kleinen Propheten* [1963⁴] 176). Haggai asks how the people have got on hitherto (if the Septuagint correctly represents the meaning of the ancient text with the question "How did you fare?" [see textual note **16a-a**]). Haggai answers the question himself: in two parallel sentences, he defines what has been hitherto as a time of disappointment. More precisely than in 1:6, 9a, 10f., he describes the disproportion between expectation and actual results in the grain and grape harvest. On the heaps of grain cf. Ruth 3:7. Only half the amount of grain expected had been harvested (and grain was the staple foodstuff) and no more than two-fifths of the wine that had been hoped for. יקב is the vessel or basin which held the juice that had been pressed out; it ran into this basin through a pipe leading from the treading floor (see textual note **16c**). For Haggai, only the relationship between the figures is important—the discrepancy between expectation and harvest. The Septuagint and the Vulgate add the actual measures: εἴκοσι σάτα—δέκα σάτα, 20 to 10 Hebrew measures of grain; πεντήκοντα μετρητάς, 50 pitchers; *viginti modiorum,* 20 bushels; *quinquaginta lagoenas,* 50 wine flasks. Thus Haggai first of all energetically exhorts the people to remember the distress they have experienced hitherto.

[2:17] Verse 17 has been interpolated later (see p. 62 above), and continues to make the same point in a different style. It shows the reason for the poor harvests described in v. 16. By way of a divine utterance, Yahweh shows himself to be the one who has afflicted the people's grain with disease; for 17a, cf. Deut. 28:22; 1 Kings 8:37, as well as Amos 4:9. In touching on the vineyard losses, the interpolator adds hail to what Haggai says, as one cause of the damage: through the hail, Yahweh tore the vines to ribbons (Ps. 78:47). Haggai, on the other hand, put down the economic distress solely to the drought (which Yahweh had called forth; 1:10f.). In a summing up, "all the work of your hands" is added as the object of God's judgment, taking up the phrase from 2;14aβ, though in assimilation to the style of direct address used here (2nd person plural; cf. aα and b; cf. also "all the work of hands" in 1:11bβ). According to this interpolation, the purpose of all the previous ill fortune was nothing other than the people's return to Yahweh (see textual note **2:17b-b**). The fact that this has not yet taken place, explains and justifies the failure of the harvest, according to v. 16. Haggai himself had never talked about a return to Yahweh, in the sense of Amos 4:6-11 (cf. 4:4f.; 5:4f.). What he saw as a return was in line, rather, with 1 Kings 8:37ff., where return to Yahweh shows itself through a turn in prayer to the temple in Jerusalem. All that Haggai required was the building of the temple (1:8), though this was certainly linked with the expectation of Yahweh's glorious presence. The fact that according to 2:15b "stone [had now been] placed to stone on Yahweh's temple" sufficed him as sign of the return to Yahweh. It is just this, v. 17 adds, that had been lacking before.

[2:18a] Verse 18a reverts to Haggai's lively, spoken style, and repeats his spur to be attentively observant of further events, which may be expected now that work on the foundations has been taken in hand. The repetition increases the tension.

[2:18b] But before the text continues and completes the sayings uttered on the beginning of the building (v. 19), a precise explanation of "this present day" (18aβ) is interpolated in commentary style, and in two stages (18bα and β). This is unmistakably the style of a later gloss (see pp. 61f. above). The date given—the 24th day of the 9th month (= December 18)—has often been viewed as secondary and erroneous (from J. W. Rothstein [61] to W. Rudolph [46]; see textual note **18a-a**). According to this view, the original reading was לַשִּׁשִּׁי ("of the sixth") instead of לתשיעי ("of the ninth"), in line with 1:15a; and the sixth month was only replaced by the ninth in view of the present context of 2:10. But if the Haggai chronicler entered the dating in 2:18b, in accordance with 2:10, when he transposed 2:15f., 18a, 19, then we need assume only a single correction process.

The second definition of "this day" in 18bβ is a definition of its content, not a definition by the calendar. It tries to identify the date with the "placing stone to stone" in 2:15b. יסד *pi'el* and *pu'al* is not merely a precise technical term in constructional engineering for the laying and being laid of foundations. It also marks the beginning of building work generally, the laying of the lowest layer (cf. 2:15) or even, more comprehensively, the restoration of a building as a whole; cf. A. Gelston, *VT* 16 (1966); W. H. Schmidt, *ThAT* I, 736f.; R. Mosis, *ThWAT* III, 676f. and 1 Kings 5:17; 6:37; Zech. 4:9; 8:9; Ezra 3:6, 10. According to this gloss too, as well as 2:15b, work started first of all on the היכל, the great assembly hall of the temple (see p. 64 above).

With the last two words, the editor of 18b picks up the call to attentiveness from 2:15a and 18a, though in abbreviated form, in order to link up with the older text of the scene-sketch and—in the transition to the close of the address—to make the tense expectation again clearly detectable.

[2:19] In 19a we again clearly find Haggai's own, familiar, spoken, dialog style. We saw that after the first call of 2:15a a question probably initially followed ("How did you fare?" see textual note **16a-a**); and here too a העוד follows—that is to say, the rhetorical interrogative particle הֲ, which expects assent and may here be understood as a limited admission: "surely!" "certainly!"; see textual note **19a.** Like v. 16, 19a again stresses the distress that has prevailed hitherto, right up until the day of the turn of events—the day which has just been reached: "still!" Still the seed cannot be sown in the furrows; since there is no rain, it must remain in the granary (cf. Joel 1:17 and H. W. Wolff, BK XIV/2, 40 [Eng., *Joel and Amos,* 35]). The olive tree still bears no olives (19aβ). After the failure of the corn (16a, 19aα) and grape harvest (16b), the lack of oil too is now lamented, oil being the third classic crop (on corn—unfermented wine—oil see 1:11 and p. 49 above). The prophet admits that these painful privations have lasted until "the present day." The interpolator even expands the list of poor harvests, adding to the olive trees, vines, fig trees, and pomegranates. (See p. 62 above and textual note **19b-b.**)

But "from this day on I will bless." The prophet announces the turn to blessing abruptly (see textual note **19c**) and as tersely as possible. Up to now, two demands for attentiveness (15a, 18a) have been followed merely by a reminder of the previous dreadful results of the drought (16, 19a), so that only tense expectation of the future has been excited: the expectation itself—an expectation of something new and impending—was not given any precise form. Now, however, in the last sentence, with its brief "I will bless," everything is said—everything that is going to change the situation "from this day onward" and in the future. The curse about which Haggai had to remind his hearers in his first discourse (1:6, 9-11) is ended. The blessing makes the failed harvests, the drought, and all the resulting want and privation a thing of the past. The blessing brings with it the means of life. The turn to blessing comes from Yahweh's own assurance.

Purpose and Thrust

Haggai's second discourse (2:15f., 18a, 19), held three and one-half weeks after his first appeal (1:15a, cf. 1:12-14), accompanies the beginning of work on the temple foundations (2:15b). It is a passionate exhortation to discover this day as the end of the farmers' previous distress and as the beginning of a new era of blessing. The Deuteronomic, 70-times repeated "Now" (cf. Deut. 5:1-3; 7:9-11; 8:19; Ps. 95:7b and H. W. Wolff, *Anthropologie,* 132-135 [Eng., *Anthropology,* 86-88]) here takes on a new meaning, as the reversal point, or pivot, between yesterday and tomorrow. From today on, something is to come about that never was before. Three times Haggai's listeners are exhorted to perceive with sharpened perceptions that "from this day on" (2:15a, 18a, [bβ], 19b) and in the time to follow, things will not remain as they had been. The person who hears will be able to observe that from one day to another—from today to tomorrow—living conditions will change for the better. "This sharp fixation of the Now is characteristic of the realism of the salvation-history thinking of these prophets (Hag. 2:15, 18; Zech. 8:11)" (G. von Rad, *Theologie des Alten Testaments* II, 296f. [cf. Eng., *Old Testament* Theology II, 286]).

The conditions for the change are worthy of note. At first sight, human decision is determinative—the decision on this day "to place stone to stone on Yahweh's temple" (2:15b; cf. 18bβ). Without a particular human act, nothing would change. But this act is an act of obedience to the prophetic demand (1:8a), and springs from the divine influence on human will (1:12-14). The obedience is a festal act rather than a human achievement. So it is not the act as such that brings about the new era: it is the recognition of God's judgment (1:9-11) and trust in God's promise (1:8b). The harvests failed and distress prevailed in spite of human effort. The drought could not be averted by anything that human beings could do. And in the same way, the turn to blessing is not the result of the farmers' exertions. It comes from the One who disposes over both drought and fertility. The real condition for new fertility is therefore the expectation of God's glorious presence in the sanctuary. But the people do not have to wait until the temple has been completed, as might perhaps be expected. The very first hand that is laid to the foundations counts, and already suffices. The promise of blessing, that is to say, is not dependent on achievement. The only human precondition required is trust.

The Haggai chronicler sees the matter in a somewhat different light when, in a literary intervention, he places the discourse in 2:15-19* immediately after 2:10-14, and sets it in the context of a new "Now" (on 2:15aα see pp. 61ff. above). "Now" the condition for the turn to blessing is the refusal to let "the unclean" participate in the building of the temple (see p. 95 below on 2:14).

For the Haggai chronicler as for the prophet himself, the decisive message in 2:15-19* remains: "From this day on I will bless." This אברך ("I will bless") deserves a reflection of its own. Often though the word *blessing* is used in the Old Testament, the form we find in this passage— ברך *pi'el*, 1st person singular— is unique; cf. J. Scharbert, "ברך, *ThWAT* I, 826f. Here and here alone the verb is uttered by Yahweh's own "I," and without any object. (Cf. Ps. 115:12, where it is also without an object, but appears in the 3rd person.) Of course, the promise is intended to be understood first of all in a quite material sense (in the light of vv. 16 and 19a): "I will bring about the blessings of harvest." But this also means: "I will confer vitality and a peaceful future." Yet paraphrases of this kind say too little by saying too much. In the objectless self-promise, Israel's God confers his own presence, which itself blesses. In this way the saying is also an interpretation of 1:8b. No solemn words of blessing are uttered or spelled out. "I will bless": that says more.

Thus the assurance of blessing can spread its ripples far beyond that early postexilic community—beyond even Israel itself (Isa. 51:2; 61:9) to the further reaches of the world of the Gentiles (Isa. 19:25). The New Testament community can ultimately also learn from Haggai's second discourse. This is her God and Lord, from whom she too can expect help in material distress. She too should concern herself with the specific, material place where she is gathered in his presence. But since Jesus' crucifixion, God's presence and the blessing it confers must not be sought primarily in terms of material prosperity. "Seek first the kingdom of God and his righteousness, and all these things shall be yours as well" (Matt. 6:33). The community working on the foundation that is both old and new should also watch attentively for the change in the time to come, as the repeated call here demands (2:15, 18). She should expect, not this thing or that, but the presence of her Lord, who blesses.

Third Scene:
The Raising Up of the Assailed

Literature

G. von Rad, "Die Stadt auf dem Berge," *EvTh* 8 (1948/49) 439-447 = his *Gesammelte Studien*, TB 8 (1958, 1971⁴) 214-224. G. Krause, "Aller Heiden Trost, Haggai 2,7. Die Beweggründe für eine falsche Übersetzung und Auslegung des Textes durch Luther," *Solange es Heute heisst: Fests. R. Herrmann* (1957) 170-178. H. A. Brongers, "Bemerkungen zum Gebrauch des adverbialen *weᵉattāh* im Alten Testament," *VT* 15 (1965) 289-299. W. A. M. Beuken, *Haggai—Sacharja 1–8. Studien zur Überlieferungsgeschichte der frühnachexilischen Prophetie*, SSN 10 (1967) 49-64. L. Tetzner, "Die rabbinischen Kommentare zum Buche Haggai," diss. Munich (1969). M. A. Dandamaev, *Persien unter den ersten Achämeniden*, Beiträge zur Iranistik 8 (1976). R. A. Mason, "The Purpose of the 'Editorial Framework' of the Book of Haggai," *VT* 27 (1977) 413-421. E. J. Bickerman, "La seconde année de Darius," *RB* 88 (1981) 23-28. R. Borger, *Die Chronologie des Darius-Denkmals am Behistun-Felsen*, NAWG (1982) 103-132. W. Schottroff, "Zur Sozialgeschichte Israels in der Perserzeit," *VF* 27 (1982) 46-68. R. Borger and W. Hinz, "Die Behistun-Inschrift Darius' des Grossen," *TUAT* I/4 (1984) 419-450.

Text

1:15b   In the second year of Darius the king,

2:1   in the seventh (month), on the twenty-first (day) of the month, the word of Yahweh came through[a] the prophet Haggai, saying:

2   Speak to Zerubbabel, the son of Shaltiel,[a] the governor of Judah,[b] and to Joshua, the son of Jehozadak, the high priest, and to[c] the remnant of the people, saying:

3 Who is left among you
        who saw this house in its former glory?
    And how do you see it now?
        Is it not in your eyes as[a] nothing?

4 Yet now stand fast, Zerubbabel!—[a]saying of Yahweh.[a]
    [Stand fast, Joshua, son of Jehozadak, high priest!]
    Stand fast, all you people of the land!—[a]saying of Yahweh.[a]
        And work!
    For I am with you—[a]saying of Yahweh of hosts.[a]

5 —[a][Together with the word that I agreed with you
        when you came out of Egypt][a]—
    My Spirit remains constantly in your midst.
        Fear not!

6 For thus has Yahweh of hosts spoken:
    [a]It is only a little while,[a]
        then I will shake heaven and earth,
            [b]sea and dry land.

7 I will shake all nations.
        The treasures[a] of all nations shall come,
    And I will fill this house with[b] glory,
        Yahweh of hosts has said.

8 To me[a] belongs silver,[b]
    to me[a] belongs gold[b]
        —saying of Yahweh of hosts.

9 Great will be the glory of this house,
        (greater) the future[a] (glory) than the former,
            Yahweh has said.
    And in this place I will confer[b] salvation
        —saying of Yahweh.
    [c][Namely, salvation of soul (saving of life) for the strengthening of
    everyone who helps to build this temple].[c]

2:1a The Haggai fragment from Murabbaʿat (*Discoveries in the Judaean Desert* II, 203)
reads אל ("to") here instead of ביד ("through"). Mur is thereby assimilating to 2:10 and 20
(cf. also Zech. 1:1, 7; 6:9; 7:1). אל is an understandable factual correction, since in what
follows (v. 2) the prophet himself is addressed first of all (אמר־נא, "speak!"). It is in v. 3
for the first time that the recipient of the word (אל, "to") becomes its mediator (2:1, ביד,
"through"). All the same, אל־חגי "to Haggai" (1bβ) before the triple אל of the recipients
of the oracle in v. 2 is improbable as the original reading (although see 2:20-21). אל instead
of ביד in 1bβ is the single variant worth mentioning in the Haggai fragment from
Murabbaʿat, which contains the text from 1:12 to 2:10. Gk ἐν χειρὶ Ἀγγαίου, "through
Haggai's agency," and Targ ביד confirm MT.

2a See textual note **1:12b** above.

2b On the Gk variant see textual note **1:1b** above.

2c Gk πάντας, "all" (also S) presupposes כל, as in 1:12, 14 (cf. also 2:4). Vg *ad reliquos
populi*, "to the rest of the people," and Targ ולשארא דעמא confirm MT. Cf. also Zech.
8:6, 11, which are without כל ("all").

3a   Cf. Gen. 44:18; Lev. 7:7; Isa. 24:2 and BrSynt §109d; Joüon, *Gr* §174i; H. W. Wolff, BK XIV/1, 103 (Eng., *Hosea,* 82).

4a-a   *Biblia Hebraica Stuttgartensia* considers omitting the phrase. But MT is supported by Gk, Targ, and Vg.

5a-a   The grammatical relationship of the supplementary clauses introduced by את can be one of three. (1) They are a later-added object for עשׂו (''perform'') in 4aδ. This is the way Vg interprets it: *et facite … verbum quod placui vobiscum cum egrederemini de terra Aegypti* (''and perform … the word which I promised you when you departed from the land of Egypt''). It is also in line with rabbinic tradition: ''Ibn Ezra: ועשׂו [''and do'' or ''perform''] is connected with the beginning of the following verse, that is with את־הדבר [''the word''] and the sense is, to keep and practice the biblical precepts''; similarly David Kimchi, according to L. Tetzner (*Rabbinische Kommentare,* 31). (2) It is a way of interpreting אני־אתכם (''I am with you'') in 4bα, though this would be unusual. (3) It is an interpretation of 5aβ. This would be very close to Isa. 59:21, in tense, language, and theology alike. The assurance of the support of the Spirit is founded on the reminder of the word of the covenant given at the Exodus. At all events, 5aα must be seen as an interpolation, for it is still unknown to Gk, Old Latin (Sabatier) and Sy^h and interrupts the parallel assurances of support in 4b and 5aβ. It is probably to the last of these to which it should be related.

6a-a   The unusual four-term announcement of an impending threat expands the more frequent two-term formula עוד מעט (''in a short time,'' ''in only a little,'' ''soon''; Hos. 1:4; Isa. 10:25; Jer. 51:33; Ps. 37:10; Exod. 17:4). Gk ἔπι ἅπαξ, ''yet again,'' presupposes only two words here also. אחת underlines the uniqueness of the ''little while'' (KBL³, 30). היא (''it'') is an announcement of the event which is further developed in what follows. A. S. van der Woude considers the textual problems in detail. Cf. also P. R. Ackroyd, *Exile* (1968), 153f. W. Rudolph takes a different view, interpreting ''this once,'' ''once more,'' following Gk.

6b   A fragment from the Cairo genizah and some other individual manuscripts read את (particle indicating the object) instead of ואת. The omission of the copula (''and''), which also determines the rhythm, is probably the original reading, since it is irregular.

7a   The singular can have a collective meaning (''what is precious''). But in view of the plural verb ובאו ''and will come,'' and the plural form of the Gk τὰ ἐκλεκτὰ (''choice things''), the plural vocalization חֲמֹדֹת (''treasures'') is to be preferred; cf. P. R. Ackroyd, *Exile;* Ges. K. §145e; KBL³ 312f. On the other hand Vg, Targ, and S presuppose the MT reading. Vg interprets the clause in a messianic sense: *et veniet Desideratus cunctis gentibus* (cf. AV: ''and the desire of all nations shall come''). This interpretation sees a correspondence between 2:21b-23 and 2:6bα-7aβ.

7b   For the double accusative cf. 1 Sam. 16:1; Isa. 33:5.

8a   The anteposition of the predicate (preposition with noun or pronoun) in the nominal clause is strongly emphatic; cf. Ps. 24:1; 31:15a and Joüon, *Gr* §154f.

8b   In Hebrew the names of species and materials are always given the definite article; cf. BrSynt §21cβ.

9a   האחרון, ''the latter,'' can be related to כבוד, ''glory'' as in Gk ἡ δόξα τοῦ οἴκου τούτου ἡ ἐσχάτη (''the latter glory of this house'') or to הבית הזה, ''this house'' (Vg: *gloria domus istius novissimae,* ''the glory of this newest house''); cf. BrSynt §21c. The general trend of the utterance speaks in favor of Gk.

9b   S makes the point clearer still: *my* salvation.

9c-c   Gk offers an explanatory addition: καὶ εἰρήνην ψυχῆς εἰς περιποίησιν παντὶ τῷ κτίζοντι τοῦ ἀναστῆσαι τὸν ναὸν τοῦτον "and peace of soul for the strengthening of all who help to build this temple." It therefore restricts the promise explicitly to those individuals who help in the temple building, and narrows down the meaning of שָׁלוֹם to "peace of soul" (saving of life?).

Form

Externally, this passage is clearly distinguished as a separate section by the dates in the introductory sentences 1:15b—2:1 (see p. 59 above) and in 2:10. In content too the series of oracles can easily be seen as a self-contained whole, dominated as it is from v. 3 to v. 9 by the theme of "the former glory of the house" compared with its present and its future glory (עתה .... הבית הזה בכבודו הראשון [v. 3] כבוד הבית הזה האחרון מן־הראשון [v. 9]).

    The development takes four forms, or stages. The passage begins as a disputation, with (1) questions which enter into the people's disappointment (v. 3). These questions are followed (2) by exhortations (v. 4a) which set the "but now" (ועתה, v. 4aα) of encouragement over against the "now" (עתה, v. 3bα) of the temple ruins. The exhortation "have courage!" is backed up by two reasons: first (stage 3 in the development) by two different assurances of support (4b, 5aβ, b) introduced by כי, "for," "because," in 4bα; second (stage 4) by three promises of Yahweh's glorious help (introduced by כי, "for," "because," in 6aα) which is to be expected in the near future (6-7, 9a.b). These three promises are separated from one another by the formula for a divine saying and by the messenger formula, and also include a didactic statement or precept (v. 8).

    All in all, therefore, we do not find here what form criticism would see as a self-contained discourse. What we have are rhetorically distinct groups of sayings, generally composed of several different parts, which in their present literary complex also display clumsy or disjointed transitions, for example from 3 to 4 and from 5 to 6. It would therefore seem plausible to see the literary structure of the oracles in vv. 3-9 as here too representing the sketch of a scene in which Haggai appeared, a sketch deriving from the group of the prophet's pupils or disciples (see p. 33 above).

    In this passage too the editorial intervention, or redaction, of the Haggai chronicler is clearly distinguishable from the scene-sketch. It can be most easily recognized (parallel to 1:1-3, 12a, 14; see pp. 31f. above) in the introduction to the confronting event of the word (1:15b—2:1), which is here furnished with a special charge to the messenger (2:2:[נא־]אמר, "[now] speak!", as in 2:21), with the names of those to whom the message is addressed. It is a question whether the Haggai chronicler has modified the scene-sketch he was using as copy apart from this. Because of the various addressees named in 2:2, the gaze is bound to pass rapidly on to v. 4.

    In the comparison, the point that strikes the reader most is that here "all the people of the land" are named (v. 4), instead of "the remnant of the people," as in v. 2. The difference is reminiscent of the distinction between "the people" in the first prophetic scene-sketch (1:12b, 13a; cf. 1:2) and "all the remnant of the people" in the Haggai chronicle (1:12a, 14a). Haggai probably originally wanted to make the group of builders as wide as possible. That is why he talks here about "the whole people of the land" (כל, "all," "entire," is missing in 1:12b, 13a). Here he no doubt includes the returned exiles ("the remnant of the people"), but he certainly did not, for the time being, wish to exclude the old, established Judaeans who were living in and round about Jerusalem. The Haggai chronicler, on the other hand, sees only "the remnant of the people" as addressed, according to 2:2, and he restricts the group (in accord with 2:14) to "the clean" (see p. 92 below). This is in line with his intention in cutting away the second scene (now 2:15-19) from 1:15a, and putting it after scene four (2:10-14). (On ועתה, "but now," in 2:15 see p. 61 above.)

The address to "the whole people of the land" therefore certainly belongs to Haggai's own words. Equally certainly, the address to Joshua, the son of Jehozadak, the high priest, in v. 4 is a resumption of the highly official language of the Haggai chronicler (cf. v. 2). The fact that at the end of the address to Joshua the divine-oracle formula נאם יהוה ("saying of Yahweh") is missing, although it is included in the sayings addressed to Zerubbabel and "the entire people of the land," suggests that this line was added later.

Where to assign the address to Zerubbabel is a difficult question. Certain points suggest that it belongs to the original scene-sketch: (1) his father's name and his official title are missing (though these are given in the case of the high priest); (2) the title "governor of Judah" is also missing in the form of address used in the early Haggai text in 2:23; and (3) the assurance closes, like the assurance to "the entire people of the land," with נאם יהוה ("saying of Yahweh"), which is not the case in the address to Joshua. Yet it is impossible to assign the address to the original Haggai oracle with complete certainty; for, in the first place, it is not only in 2:23 that the official title is missing. It is also lacking in the chronicler's account in 1:12a (see p. 51 above). Moreover, in the light of the questions in v. 3, it is really only an address to the people that makes sense; for Zerubbabel, like Joshua, was born in exile (see p. 38 above), and cannot therefore have been numbered among the witnesses to the first temple.

With the exception of 1:15b—2:2, therefore, it is only the address to Joshua in v. 4a that can with certainty be assigned to the editorial additions of the Haggai chronicler. But the possibility that the address to Zerubbabel was one of these additions cannot be entirely ruled out.

Setting

The questions in v. 3 show that the setting of this series of sayings also must be looked for in direct proximity to the temple ruins.

Verse 1 names the 21st day of the 7th month as the date of the scene. It is the 7th day of the Feast of Tabernacles, the great autumn festival, which begins on the 15th day of the 7th month (Lev. 23:34; Num. 29:12). Since absolute cessation of work was enjoined for the 8th day, the last day of the festival (Lev. 23:36, 39; Num. 29:35), we find ourselves on the last day but one before work was resumed on the temple. (On the sacrifices to be offered on the 7th day, cf. Num. 29:32-34.) It is October 17 in the second year of Darius's reign. What year was that, according to our Gregorian calendar?

Excursus: The Second Year of Darius

The Haggai chronicler dates all the prophet's oracles "in the second year of Darius" (1:1; 1:15b; and 2:10). According to this, Haggai's utterances fell within the space of less than four months, on the 1st day of the 6th month, the 24th day of the 6th month, the 21st day of the 7th month and the 24th day of the 9th month. What has recently become a point of chronological controversy is whether these months belonged to 520 or to 521. The answer is linked with a kerygmatic problem: what is the relationship between certain points in Haggai's proclamation (particularly 2:6f. and 2:21-23) and events in the Persian Empire, especially in the second year of Darius's reign?

E. J. Bickerman discusses this problem in "En marge de l'écriture II. La seconde année de Darius," *RB* 88 (1981) 23-28. In recent years the generally accepted opinion has been that Haggai made his appearance in the year 520. But Bickerman takes another view, maintaining that the year must have been 521. The most recent consideration of the decisive text, however, still comes down on the side of 520: see R. Borger and W. Hinz, "Die Behistun-Inschrift Darius' des Grossen," *TUAT* I/4 (1984) 419-450; cf. also R. A. Parker and W. H. Dubberstein, *Babylonian Chronology* 626 B.C.—A.D. 75 (1956) 14-16 and M. A. Dandamaev, *Persien* (1956) 114ff.

The Behistun inscription (§§11-13) makes it certain—and about this there is no dispute—that after the Gaumâta's revolt against Cambyses on the 14th day of the 12th month (= March 11, 522) and his seizure of power over the whole empire on the 9th day of the 4th month (= July 1, 522), Darius crushed the rebels "with a few men on the 10th day of the 7th month" (= September 29, 522) and himself took over the government of the Persian Empire on the same day. The full year ran from March 27, 522, until April 13, 521 (it was a leap year; see *TUAT* I/4, 443).

What is a matter of controversy, on the other hand, is the numbering of the years of Darius I's reign. Should the whole year when he took over the government (522/521) be counted as the first year of his reign, even though he only became ruler of the whole empire on the 10th day of the 7th month (September 29, 522), thus making the 2nd year of his reign already begin with the new calendar year on April 14, 521? In this case the 21st day of the 7th month (Hag. 2:1) would correspond to October 28, 521, and the 24th day of the 9th month (Hag. 2:10, 20) would correspond to December 30, 521 (Bickerman's view, 26). Or, alternatively, should the year when Darius took over government—the year of his accession—be assigned to the rule of this predecessor, so that the 2nd year of Darius's reign should be counted only from the spring of 520 until the spring of 519? In this case the 21st day of the 7th month (in Hag. 2:1) would correspond to October 17, 520, and the 24th day of the 9th month (in Hag. 2:10, 20) would be December 18, 520. This is the point at issue.

The main arguments in favor of 521/20 as being the second year of Darius I's reign are as follows (according to Bickerman):

1. The year 522/21 must not be counted merely as the year of Darius's accession. It must be considered the first full year of his reign, because the government of a rebel, "the lying king" Gaumâta, does not count (Bickerman, 25). Gaumâta "lied to the people, saying: 'I am Smerdis (Bardiya), Cyrus's son, Cambyses' brother' " (Behistun §11). Darius, on the other hand, could count himself the legitimate heir of Cambyses (529–522), since Cambyses died at the beginning of July 522 in Syria, on his return from Egypt, without

leaving a son. Since the reign of the rebel Gaumâta was illegitimate (see above), the whole year 522/21 must count as Darius's first year, and 521/20 as his second.

2. In Bickerman's view, the political situation in the world accorded more closely with Haggai's sayings in 521 than it did in 520. In the months of October to December 520 the rule of Darius I over an empire reaching from the Nile to the Indus was firmly established and had long ceased to be disputed; cf. also M. A. Dandamaev, op. cit., 95. At all events, there can no longer have been any talk about dangerous revolts by other ''lying kings.'' The shaking of kingdoms and the world of the nations, which is obliquely referred to in Hag. 2:7, 22, was in 520 a thing of the past. Darius rightly boasted that ''in a single year'' he had fought 19 battles and taken 9 kings captive (Behistun §52); see on this R. Borger, *Chronologie*, NAWG (1982) 122ff., with the charts between pp. 118 and 119; photographs in the *Oxford Bible Atlas* (1974²) 30; J. B. Pritchard, *The Ancient Near East in Pictures* (1954), no. 249; M. A. Dandamaev, op. cit., Pl. II. That glorious ''single year''—in which the Gaumâta rebellion (March 11 to September 29, 522) was not included—ran from December 522 to December 521. In that period Darius put down no fewer than 9 revolts— some of them repeated—in Babylonia, Elam, Armenia, Media, Parthia, and Persia. In the autumn of 521 the violent unrest (Hag. 2:7aα) in ''the 23 countries'' (Behistun §6) of the Persian empire was still a live issue, even if the turmoil was dying down. But in the autumn of 520 the revolts may be considered a thing of the past. In October/December 520, the Persian governor Zerubbabel would immediately have clapped into prison any fanatic who had stood up in Jerusalem and announced the collapse of the empire ''in just a little while'' (Hag. 2:6). This, at least, is Bickerman's view (p. 24).

3. A prophet was not merely anxious to pick up the latest news; in the Persian period he was well able to do so. A comparison between Hag. 2:6f., 21-23 and Zech. 1:7, 11 shows how rapidly prophets in the early postexilic period drew on up-to-date information. In December, people in Jerusalem were still hoping for a worldwide upheaval (Hag. 2:6, 22), while by the following February—after barely two months—the revolutionaries had become dreamers of dreams, resigned to the failure of their utopias (Zech. 1:7, 11). In Bickerman's view (p. 27), this fits the winter of 521/20. People heard about the turn of events within a period of 8 weeks, thanks to Darius I's excellent news policy and the central courier service he built up. The great texts of the Behistun inscription, which proclaim Darius's triumphal victories, were sent out in rapid succession and in countless copies ''on clay tablets and parchment'' ''into every country; the people got to know them'' (Behistun §70). What is more, they read them in Elamite, Babylonian, Old Persian, or Imperial Aramaic, according to their requirements. Jewish soldiers in Elephantine on the Nile were able to read them, for example, since fragments in Imperial Aramaic have been found there. And we may safely assume that in Haggai's day Jerusalem was not at the end of the line as regards news contacts. We have evidence of correspondence with the exiles in Babylon from the time of Jeremiah (chap. 29); after Cambyses' Egyptian campaigns (525–522) there was a particularly brisk interchange between the southwest fringes of the Persian empire and its Asiatic centers. So Zerubbabel, the governor of Judah, will also have been swiftly and comprehensively informed in any given case. But this means that the second year of Darius's reign would more probably have been the year of the great revolts, that is to say, 521/20.

According to Bickerman, therefore, a correction to the theory about the year of Darius's accession to the throne, the situation in the empire, and the rapid flow of news to Jerusalem could all speak in favor of 521 as the year in which Haggai delivered his message. And yet, other facts speak against this view.

1. With regard to the year of Darius's accession to the throne: In 522/21 Darius I took over full power only on September 29, 522, when Gaumâta was killed (Behistun §13). Gaumâta had only assumed official rule on July 1, 522, with his fraudulent claim that he was Smerdis (Bardiya), Cambyses' brother (Behistun §12). It was merely his rebellion that had been under way ever since March 11, 522. Cambyses was the legitimate ruler of the empire until his death at the beginning of July (Behistun §11); he had heard about Gaumâta's revolt

in April 522, when he was in Egypt, and had immediately set out on a campaign against him, but died of blood poisoning at Hamath in Syria at the beginning of July, after a self-inflicted wound (W. Hinz, article "Kambyses," *Reallexikon der Assyriologie* V [1976-80] 329; M. A. Dandamaev, op. cit., maintains a different view; see here W. Schottroff, "Sozialgeschichte ... in der Perserzeit," *Verkündigung und Forschung* 27 [1982] 51f.). Even if—in the context of Gaumâta's claim—we could (with Bickerman's arguments) dispute the date of Darius's accession to the throne (on the grounds that Gaumâta was merely an illegitimate claimant), we must at all events take into account the legitimacy of Cambyses' rule up to the beginning of July 522. In no case can the whole of the year 522/21 be counted as the first year of Darius's reign. Properly speaking, it was the last year of the reign of Cambyses, and accordingly the year of Darius's accession. This means that, since Darius acceded to the throne on September 29, 522, the accession year ran until April 13, 521, and the first full year of his reign from April 14, 521, to March 3, 520. The second year then begins on March 4, 520 (R. A. Parker and W. H. Dubberstein, *Babylonian Chronology;* 30).

2. With regard to the political situation: It is true that in this second year of Darius's reign the pacification of the empire had, largely speaking, been completed. But Darius himself reports in addenda dated 518 (Behistun §71) that "in the second and third year after he had become king" a revolt in Elam had to be put down, and later a Scythian rebellion (Behistun §73). So there was a degree of unrest in 520 as well.

3. As for the flow of information: We may undoubtedly assume that people in Jerusalem were informed relatively accurately and rapidly about events in the empire. But even if we leave on one side the striking dating "in the second year of King Darius" (1:1, 15b; 2:10)—which suggests that his rule was undisputed—we must still note and explain in detail the completely divergent treatment of the theme "world revolution" in the Behistun inscription and in Hag. 2:6-9, 21-23. This divergence also relativizes the importance of the question whether Haggai made his public appearance in 521 or 520, even if the later date would seem certain. The theme of Yahweh's shaking of the world of the nations is not disposed of just because the rule of a human sovereign had been stabilized.

Commentary

[1:15b—2:1] The 21st day of the 7th month therefore must be understood, not as October 28, 521 (see p. 74 above), but as October 17, 520. Four weeks had past since the beginning of work on the temple foundations. Haggai may have had a double reason for speaking a third time. The great eight-day autumn festival (see pp. 73f. above) was always also an occasion for remembering the day when Solomon brought the ark into the first temple, and hence the day of that first temple's consecration; cf. 1 Kings 8:1-3, 65f. In addition, we may conclude from what Haggai says that the first weeks, and the experience of laborious and tedious work on the ruins, had spread discouragement and listlessness. The prophet seizes the traditional opportunity offered by the feast to counter the acute decline of enthusiasm.

[2:2] The Haggai chronicler tells us that these sayings were addressed not only to the responsible leaders of the community, Zerubbabel and Joshua, as was the case in Haggai's first discourse (1:1). He now also names as recipients "the remnant of the people" (that is to say, the homecomers from the gola; see pp. 51f. above). It is these people who are called to undertake the building. This was not yet the case in 1:1. According to 1:12a, 14, they have shown themselves to be obedient listeners to the prophetic call, and its willing followers, and are the people who have been really legitimated out of "the entire people of the land" (cf. 2:4 and p. 73 above). It is noticeable that here there is no longer any talk about the "whole" (כל) remnant, as there is in 1:12a, 14. This already bothered the Septuagint (see textual note to 2c). But the simple phrase שארית העם, "the remnant of the people," is normal usage (Zech. 8:6, 11, 12; Neh. 7:71; cf. Mic. 5:7; 7:18 and H. W. Wolff, *Micha,* BK XIV/4, 205).

[2:3] Haggai's sayings begin again, as in 1:4 and 2:15f., in address style, as he challenges the attitude of his listeners. Even more markedly than before, three questions, with a triple 2nd person plural address, display a passionate attempt to make contact (מי בכם—מה אתם—חלא ... בעיניכם). In each of the three questions what is under discussion is a single theme: the temple (הבית הזה, "this house"), as in 1:4 and 2:15—or here, more precisely, its "glory" (כמהו—אתו—כבודו). The first question challenges the people who can still remember Solomon's temple; the second asks about the present state of affairs; the third inquires about the consequence.

Who are "the ones who are left"? They are the survivors who were old enough for pictures of Solomon's temple to have been indelibly imprinted on their minds before the temple burned down in 587., and who now, in the year 520, are still able to participate in the crowd gathered round Haggai. They must therefore have been more than 70 years old. The governor Zerubbabel and the high priest Joshua were certainly not among this number, since they were both born in exile (see pp. 38ff. above). Whether Haggai himself was one of these old people does not emerge from his questions. The second and third of these questions show that he was reckoning with a small group of elderly eyewitnesses; otherwise these questions would be pointless. Ezra 3:12 seems to take up and develop Haggai's first question: this report describes the elderly group as being composed of "priests and Levites and heads of fathers' houses, old men who had seen the first house with their own eyes." According to Ezra 3:10-13, these people wept over the beginnings of the building work, whereas the younger ones were jubilant.

Haggai is moved by the question about the כבוד, the "glory," of the old temple. Here he is not talking about the entry of "Yahweh's glory" (cf. 1 Kings 8:11; Exod. 40:34f.; cf. Hag. 1:8 אכבד, "I will glorify myself"). Here כבוד simply means the splendor of the temple building, just as the word כבוד can be used for the "glory" of a tree (Ezek. 31:18) or a forest (Isa. 10:18), like the forests of Lebanon (Isa. 60:13), or can mean the "magnificence" and "beauty" of a rich man's house (Ps. 49:16f.; cf. 2 Chron. 32:27). If the present ruins—on which the work of a few weeks had made but little impression—were compared with the former glory of the temple, the result was deeply depressing—indeed, nothing at all. With הלא, "is not?" the questioner claims the attention of his listeners and reckons with assent. He refers to the observations of the old people themselves ("in your eyes"). A comparison follows with כ ... כ; see textual note 3a. Targum Rashi translates: "It" (the temple) and "nothing" are alike (L. Tetzner,

Rabbinische Kommentare, 30). Zechariah too (4:10) knows all about the depressing assessment of "small beginnings." Later the building of the walls is subjected to similar mockery: "Will they revive the stones out of the heaps of rubbish?" (Neh. 3:34). Haggai knows the difficulty of every new start. The questions he puts show his sympathy. But he is aware of, and resists, the danger of letting the bleak and disconsolate findings of the elderly undermine the vigor and enthusiasm of the people who are working on the building.

[2:4]   With וְעַתָּה ("but now," v. 4), he confronts the "now" of the pitiable situation (v. 3) with a new "now" of encouragement. Here וְעַתָּה positively acquires the flavor of an "in spite of that" or a "nonetheless." In Isa. 64:7, similarly, the phrase introduces an act of confidence, in defiance of an adverse situation (H. A. Brongers, *VT* 15 [1965] 295; cf. also earlier Hag. 1:5; 2:15). A triple divine saying justifies this "nonetheless" of encouragement (twice נְאֻם־יְהוָה, "saying of Yahweh," in 4aα, γ and a closing נְאֻם־יְהוָה צְבָאוֹת, "saying of Yahweh Sebaoth" in bβ; see p. 100 below, excursus).

On the revision of the scene-sketch in v. 4, see pp. 72f. above.

Here Zerubbabel is not addressed as "governor of Judah," as if his authority were derived from the Persian king (cf. in contrast 1:1, 14; 2:2). He is addressed simply by name (cf. 1:12; 2:23). As the man who listens to Yahweh's voice (1:12a) and as the person who, as Yahweh's servant, enjoys his particular confidence (2:23), he is responsible before all others for the enthusiasm of the temple building team. The high priest is only at his side in a secondary capacity. But the assurance is addressed above all to the assembled community, which has already been addressed in v. 3 (see p. 77 above).

Whom does Haggai mean with "the people of the land in their entirety"? The meaning of this expression apparently shifted in the course of history. In preexilic days, עַם־הָאָרֶץ ("the people of the land") meant the upper class, citizens in the fullest sense—the people who were landowners and political leaders; cf. 2 Kings 11:14ff.; 21:24; 23:30 and E. Würthwein, *Der 'amm ha'arez im Alten Testament* (1936) 53. In the postexilic period, on the other hand, Ezra 4:4 means by עַם־הָאָרֶץ the enemies of the עַם־יְהוּדָה, "people of Judah," or "the enemies of Judah and Benjamin" (4:1a). This עַם־הָאָרֶץ ("people of the land") is distinguished particularly from the בְּנֵי הַגּוֹלָה, "the sons of the gola" (4:1b), who took up the building of the temple under Zerubbabel and Joshua and who here too are termed the "remnant" (שְׁאָר "remnant," that is, of the heads of families, Ezra 4:3). The people belonging to this עַם־הָאָרֶץ were descended from the non-Israelites who had been settled there by the king of Assyria after the fall of the Northern Kingdom (Ezra 4:2b; cf. 2 Kings 17:24-41). The people who are described here as the עַם־הָאָרֶץ would have liked to help build the temple, but they were rejected because they were for the most part of heathen origin (Ezra 4:2-3). Haggai's "people of the land" must have been somewhere between these two meanings of the phrase (see p. 73 above). According to Hag. 2:4, we can certainly not exclude the returned exiles under Zerubbabel (and Joshua) from the group working on the temple, if we assume that 2:1 offers an explanation more or less in accordance with the facts. On the other hand, in the light of preexilic linguistic usage, we must suppose that old, established Judaeans from Jerusalem, Judah, and Benjamin were also included (cf. also Zech. 7:2, 5), perhaps even together with such descendants of 8th-century Assyrian settlers as "had joined them and separated [themselves] from the pollutions of the peoples of the land" (Ezra 6:21). At all events, Haggai himself points beyond an all-too-narrow interpretation, when he emphatically addresses "the entirety" of the people of the land. Perhaps the language he uses is a sign that he himself belonged to a family which had been able to remain in the country in 587; cf. S. Amsler, CAT XIc (1981) 33; W. Rudolph, KAT XIII/4 (1976) 42; P. R. Ackroyd, *Exile* (1968) 162; R. A. Hulst, "גּוֹי/עַם, Volk," *THAT*, II, ed. E. Jenni and C. Westermann (1984³), 300f.

With his encouraging call, therefore, Haggai turns to the wider group of people concerned with the building of the temple—that is, to both homecomers and old, established Judaeans. חֲזַק (imperative *qal*), "stand fast" or "be strong," demands that they summon up all their strength and do not lose heart. Many speeches begin with this same call (2 Sam. 13:28; Isa. 35:4; Ps. 31:24). It especially often introduces words of encouragement before the people go off to war (Deut. 31:6f.; Josh. 10:25; 2 Sam. 10:12), particularly in Deuteronomic writings and the Chronicler (Josh. 1:9; 2 Chron. 19:11; 32:7). Especially worth noting are the words of David to Solomon in Chronicles on the preparation of the temple ministry (1 Chron. 28:10, 20). Just as David once exhorted his son Solomon, so Haggai now buoys up all the people of the land (and Zerubbabel as well?). Both David and Haggai demand resolute action. The set phrase חֲזַק וַעֲשֵׂה ("Be strong and do it") is not unusual, either in the singular or in the plural (1 Chron. 28:10, 20; Ezra 10:4 and frequently). Haggai's encouragement wrests the people out of their depressive passivity and leads to the vigorous activity that is imperative for the work required. In hard fact, what is meant is simply the continuation of work on the temple. (The addition in 5aα is different; cf. textual note **5a-a**.)

[2:5] Haggai knows that one's own strength and energy is soon at an end. He therefore gives a double reason (כִּי, "because," at the beginning of 4b and 6a) why the people should be resolute and persevering: in the first place, Yahweh's promise of support (4b, 5aβ, b), secondly, the promise of his worldwide intervening acts in the imminent future (6-9).

First of all the prophet repeats Yahweh's promise: "I am at your side." This assurance was already given at the close of the first scene-sketch (1:13). For the interpretation see p. 50 above. Now Haggai counters the אַיִן ("nothing") of the old people with Yahweh's אֲנִי ("I")—the despairing "nothingness" of things as they appear, over against the "I" of the God who is present among his people.

This assurance of support is common, in a number of linguistic variations, but it is given a particular exposition in 5aβ. This exposition talks about Yahweh's

"Spirit," in which his "I," his self, becomes efficacious. In the Chronicler's history—but even earlier as well, in Isa. 42:1; 48:16; 59:21; Ezek. 11:5— Yahweh's "Spirit" is indissolubly and exclusively connected with the prophetic proclamation (cf. 2 Chron. 15:1; 18:23; 20:14; 24:20; Neh. 9:20, 30; also W. A. M. Beuken, *Studien* [1967] 57f.). רוח ("spirit") as human will power (1:14) can become the victim of dejection (2:3); but Yahweh's "Spirit" is animating vigor, strengthening presence, and encouraging authority; see pp. 52f. above). This "Spirit" is enduring and constant (on עמד, "stand," "remain enduringly," cf. Exod. 9:28; 2 Kings 6:31; Ps. 33:11) and by way of the prophets its workings are felt in the midst of the community, as they are at present, through the prophet Haggai, who encourages the despondent; cf. the saying to Zerubbabel in Zech. 4:6. So the lament of the people (touched on in v. 3) can be followed by the classic saving cry: "Fear not!" (Lam. 3:57), the cry which is so often linked with the assurance of help, as it is here (cf. for example Isa. 41:10; 43:1f.). The late addition 5aα (see textual note **2:5a-a**) elucidates the promise of the Spirit, and of support, with the word of the covenant (Torah?) given at the exodus from Egypt (cf. Jer. 31:31f.).

[2:6f.] Yahweh's enduring support, then, is the first ground for encouragement, and it is considerably reinforced by a series of promises. The first of these is clearly marked off from the others by the introductory and closing messenger formula (6aα and 7bβ respectively). The messenger saying itself is dominated by Yahweh's first person address ("I": 6b, 7aα.bα). Only one result clause (7aβ) intervenes in Yahweh's own proclamation of what he is going to do. But it is just this clause that emphasizes the link between this saying and the main theme of the scene: the path from the pitiably small beginnings the people have experienced hitherto to the future glory of the temple (cf. 7bα with 3 and 9a).

[2:6] The promise provides the reason for an imminent expectation. It is true that imminent expectation is almost the rule in prophecy, but here the "soon-ness" of the fulfillment is markedly emphasized by an unusual four-term formula; see textual note **6a-a** and H. W. Wolff, BK XIV/1, 18 (Eng., *Hosea* [1986⁴] 17). The briefness of the waiting time reduces the discontent (v. 3), heightens the encouragement (v. 4a), and lends further support to Yahweh's promise of help (vv. 4b, 5b).

What is it that is supposed to happen so soon? Worry about the temple building is going to be swallowed up in a worldwide cataclysm. Yahweh himself proclaims what he is going to do. With רעש *hiphil* (the causative form), he reports his immediately impending intervention. The word רעש initially means "earthquake" (1 Kings 19:11f.; Amos 1:1; Zech. 14:5; cf. the verbal use in Judg. 5:4; Isa. 13:13; Ps. 18:7). רעש *qal*, however, is not used only in reference to the earth. It soon comes to be applied to the heavens as well (Joel 2:10; 3:16; cf. Judg. 5:4; Ps. 68:8). This is the case primarily in the description of theophanies: heaven and earth tremble "before Yahweh." For the reminiscence of themes connected with the holy war, see pp. 102f. below. When writers talk about the heavens quaking or trembling, they are thinking specifically of thunder and lightning, tempests and cloudbursts, as well as earthquakes and flood tides, as Ps. 77:16-18 shows. In Ezek. 38:20 the sea and everything in it, as well as the birds of the heavens and the beasts of the earth, all quake "at Yahweh's presence" when there is "a great shaking in the land of Israel" (19b). In Haggai, uniquely, "sea and dry land" are put beside "heaven and earth." And here the "quaking" is no longer merely the effect of Yahweh's coming. Yahweh himself is now the actual author of the cosmic cataclysm (רעשׁ *hiphil* 6b, 7a). Yahweh makes the world quake—that is, he "shakes" the cosmos. רעשׁ *hiphil* is a rare form and, when it occurs, almost always has as its object historical forces, not natural ones—that is, "the nations" (7aα, as Ezek. 31:16), "the kingdoms" (Isa. 14:16), or "the (defeated) land of Israel" (Ps. 60:2). Haggai says that Yahweh shakes "all nations," just as he shakes the cosmic regions. Before Israel's God, nature and history, the political world and the natural environment cannot be divided. He shakes the one with the other.

Yet, surprisingly, when Haggai proclaims that Yahweh is going to "shake" the world, this is not intended to be seen as something deranging, let alone as something that destroys. It is an upheaval that leads to salvation, to a new order, which will put aside many anxieties about the building of the temple. It is astonishing how universal the upheaval is, and how particular its goal. Tumultuous military campaigns on the part of the nations of the world turn into pilgrimages to Jerusalem. The uprising of all the nations, incited and carried through by Yahweh, is going to lead to the redistribution of "the treasures of all the nations"; see textual note **7a**. What treasures are we supposed to think of? As well as the silver and gold of the following verse, we may remember other texts similar in content, such as Isa. 60:13 (which talks about costly woods, which come from Lebanon and are intended to grace the Jerusalem sanctuary) and Nah. 2:10 (silver and gold in the form of splendid appointments and vessels: כְּלִי הֶמְדָּה, "precious vessels"; cf. Hos. 13:15). The "precious vessels" which Nebuchadnezzar carried off to Babylon were those belonging to the temple (2 Chron. 36:10; cf. also Ezra 7:15f.). Among the treasures owned by Hezekiah, 2 Chron. 32:27 mentions precious stones and spices, as well as gold and silver. According to Haggai, these precious things are to be brought from all the nations for one purpose only: the Jerusalem temple. It is Yahweh himself who is going to "fill this house" with such "glory." Here as in 2:3 (see p. 77 above) כבוד means the magnificence and beauty which—when the processions from the nations arrive—will abolish all the grief and care that has prevailed hitherto; cf. Isa. 66:12 (כְּבוֹד גּוֹיִם, "splendor of the nations").

In Haggai's day, there was no lack of quite distinct ideas, whenever there was talk about revolutions in the world of the nations, or about costly gifts for the sanctuary in Jerusalem. The Persian kings Cyrus and Darius I intended that the expense of rebuilding the Jerusalem temple should be refunded from the royal treasury (Ezra 6:4, 7f.). According to Behistun §14, Darius, continuing Cyrus's policy, wished "to rebuild the sanctuaries which Gaumâta, the magus, had destroyed;

I gave back to the people the farmsteads, the cattle and the servants that Gaumâta had robbed them of.'' The Darius texts also convey an idea of what could be termed a worldwide rebellion in Haggai's day (see excursus, pp. 74-76 above). But Haggai calls upon neither Jerusalem nor Zerubbabel, the governor of Judah, to rebel (cf. Bickerman's view, p. 24, and p. 75 above). It is Yahweh, Israel's God himself, who proclaims the great upheaval. God himself is going to fill the temple with "glory" in some marvelous way—a glory far beyond everything which the builders are now so painfully missing. In this context it is quite unimportant whether the reports about revolutionary unrest in the Persian empire are one year old or two. What Haggai is announcing is not intended to extend the list of recalcitrant "lying kings." Darius's purpose was to stabilize an empire inevitably limited in time. The glorious completion of the temple is a very different goal. Haggai's purpose is also to encourage his people by setting before their eyes the acts of his God and by making them attentive to his word of promise. To reckon with the closeness of Yahweh's all-comprehending power, and with his refashioning will, is the truly reasonable attitude; and it is this that brings real encouragement.

[2:8]　Yahweh's power of disposal over all the treasures of the world is justified and impressed on the people's minds in the briefest of declarations. "Silver and gold" are the quintessence of all material values (Hos. 2:8; Ezek. 7:19; Prov. 22:1; Eccles. 2:8). The repeated pronoun לִי ("mine") which introduces the two terse nominal clauses shows where the emphasis of the statement lies (see textual note **2:8a** and cf. Ps. 24:1). This "sentence of challenging rigor" proclaims above the nations Yahweh's "sole right of possession" (G. von Rad, *EvTh* 8 [1948/49] 446 = *Gesammelte Studien,* 222). At the same time it strengthens the confidence of the disheartened. In this connection it must be stressed that what is being expressed here is not greed on Israel's part, or some kind of Jewish egoism; it is the sovereign claim of Yahweh, who turns to his impoverished people in their necessity. He does not merely act in the spheres of spirituality and eschatology. He shows that he is also the Lord of all earthly possessions and all this-worldly values. This, surely, is what his people is supposed to remember, even in their pitiful and miserable circumstances (v. 3)—or then most of all. The saying has all the impact of a tenet of faith.

[2:9a]　Thus Israel also learns to hope. For since Yahweh is the owner of everything that is of value, he has the power to change present conditions completely. The people should therefore compare the glory of Solomon's temple, not merely with the present ruins, but with what Yahweh is going to bring about in the future. Haggai picks up Deutero-Isaiah's comparison between the former (first) things and the future (last) things. But he does so in order to point, not to the correspondence between them (41:4, 21f.; 42:9; 44:6; 48:12), but to the astonishing changes that are going to come about—the change to the new thing with which the future will transform everything that has hitherto existed (cf. Isa. 43:18f.). Thus Yahweh's rule over the nations and their treasures will help the temple to arrive at a beauty hitherto unknown, so that it will be glorious to look upon. The prophet does not shrink from talking only about the outward glory first of all (on כבוד "glory," see p. 77 above); for he is vividly aware of the quite practical difficulties which are weighing so heavily on the people and making them despondent (cf. v. 3). The prophet's promise does not try to bypass or gloss over the troubles of the present, but counters them at precisely the point where they are to be found.

Excursus: The Second Temple

It was possible to consecrate the second temple in the spring of 515 (Ezra 6:15), and it was indeed by no means an insignificant building, according to the findings of contemporary research. As a whole, it was larger than Solomon's temple; the front section must have been more imposing than the vestibule of its predecessor; cf. M. A. Beek, *Geschichte Israels* (1957) 108 and T. A. Busink, *Der Tempel von Jerusalem* II (1980) 902ff. (see especially the reconstruction of Zerubbabel's temple on p. 812). Apart from a few changes made in the course of the centuries, Zerubbabel's temple lasted for exactly 500 years, until Herod the Great had its walls pulled down in the 18th year of this reign (22 B.C.), in order soon afterwards to begin the magnificent new structure, which incomparably excelled the old sanctuary in its total layout; cf. Josephus, *Jewish Antiquities* XV, 11, 1 §380 and *The Jewish War* I, 21, 1 §401.

    The last saying in the series of promises (9b) is clearly distinct from the others. Whereas the theme of these was the external appointments (כבוד) of the temple, the subject now is what can be expected from it. It is a matter of dispute, however, whether "this place" means Jerusalem, as the place of the cult, or the temple itself. Elsewhere in Haggai the temple is called "Yahweh's house" (1:2, [9], 14: בית יהוה), "this house" (2:3, 7, 9a: הבית הזה), "the house" (1:8: הבית) or "Yahweh's temple" (2:15, 18: היכל יהוה). מקום, "place," on the other hand, in comparable contexts generally means Jerusalem, as the cultic place chosen by Yahweh (Deut. 12:5; 2 Kings 22:16-20; Jer. 7:3, 7, 20 and frequently elsewhere). At the same time, in a number of prominent passages המקום הזה, "this place," is used as a synonym for הבית הזה, "this house" (1 Kings 8:29f. and 2 Chron. 6:20f., 38, 40; 7:12). That is to say, it is the precise designation for the temple. This particular interpretation is compelling here, in Haggai, in the light of the previous context. We should not therefore, like W. A. M. Beuken, *Studien*, 60-62, deny Haggai the authorship of v. 9b, viewing it as a later addition (by the Chronicler), interpolated only in the course of the transmission process. Here the place of Yahweh's glorious presence (1:8b) is, as the place of his blessing (cf. 2:15b, 19b), the place from which the divine שלום, "shalom," issues.

    In the framework of Haggai's proclamation, שלום, "shalom"—the word usually translated as "peace"—means in the first instance the "fertility" of the land, and hence the end of the curse of famine, of vain labor. What is therefore proclaimed is life that is fruitful and work that is crowned with success and satisfaction (cf. 1:6, 9-11; 2:16, 19). In the wider context we should also think of "peace" (in contrast to war)—peace throughout the world; instead of the sword the nations will bring "treasures" (cf. v. 7a with v. 22, which points to the end of all war and weapons of war). So here שָׁלוֹם means salvation in a comprehensive sense: the absence of both hunger and sword, life without privation and without enmity.

The God of Israel proclaims this healthful peace as his gift (אֶתֵּן, "I will give"), a gift he is going to confer from the completed new temple; on אֶתֵּן שָׁלוֹם, "I will give shalom," cf. Lev. 26:6; Ezek. 34:25f.; Jer. 14:13. The sanctuary is therefore not in the first instance a place from which demands or requirements issue, and to which sacrifices are to be brought. It is rather the place where Yahweh confers the preconditions for successful labor and ties between the nations of the world.

Purpose and Thrust

All the sayings in this scene have a single purpose: to overcome the weariness and disinclination of the people who are working on Yahweh's house. This had overtaken many of them, although barely a month had elapsed since the temple building had begun. The prophet suffers with his people over the scanty progress made in these first weeks. But he shows a path leading straight from "nothingness" to "glory" (vv. 3-9). The call to persevering endeavor (4a) is backed up and justified by the assurance of Yahweh's present support (4b, 5aβ, b) and then by promises of his future efficacious intervention (6-9). So "with the saying about the shabbiness of the divine beginnings, a saying that camouflages nothing, the scene takes on prophetic greatness" (G. von Rad, *Theologie des Alten Testaments* II, 292 [cf. Eng. *Old Testament Theology* II, 1965, 282]). Something new is stirring in the very midst of the poverty-stricken conditions. An important correspondence appears between the stimulating goad of the exhortation, and the divine assurance—between willing activity and eschatological event. Yahweh's presence and his future causes and conditions zeal and power to work on the sanctuary, and to endure. Anyone who, in everyday participation in God's work on earth, despairs because of the futility of what he does, may find in Haggai's third discourse a paradigm for overcoming despondency: for Haggai teaches himself not to despise "the day of small things" (Zech. 4:10). The pitiful field of ruins is shifted prophetically into the light of worldwide events (cf. v. 3 with vv. 6-9). The small, everyday act of cooperation (e.g., "fetching wood," 1:8a) and a newly won willingness and resolution (4, 5aβ, b) acquire a part in universal events (6-9). The narrowly contained pile of rubble of the Jerusalem sanctuary, on the fringes of the Persian Empire, suddenly becomes the goal and center of God's universal guidance of the nations (6f.). These nations—unexpectedly—become helpers in the adornment of the temple.

A comparison between Yahweh's worldwide revolution as Haggai saw it (6f.) with the struggles to which Darius I testifies in the Behistun inscriptions shows two things, initially. First, the notion of a great empire and the tremors that shake it to its foundations is nowhere so clearly and explicitly attested in the world of the Old Testament as it is here. Haggai knows what he is talking about when he speaks of "the shaking of all nations" (see p. 75 above). And then: Darius, like Cyrus, also allows his victories to benefit the sanctuaries of the subjected nations. It is not a mere utopia when Haggai sees "treasures from all nations" coming to Jerusalem (see p. 81 above).

Yet on closer inspection the differences are striking. It is Yahweh, Israel's God, who alone brings about the "shaking" of the nations. It is true that, in the account of his subjection of individual rebels, Darius regularly acknowledges: "Ahura Mazda helped me" (Behistun §§13, 18, 19 and frequently; cf. Haggai's acknowledgment of Yahweh's support in 2:4b, 5b). But according to Haggai, it is Yahweh himself who overthrows all the nations (2:7). In Darius's case, the individual nations are freed of their rebellious leaders and incorporated in the empire. In Haggai, the provincial city of Jerusalem and its sanctuary provide the goal for the revolt of all the nations which Yahweh is going to bring about. The whole world is to bring its treasures in honor of Yahweh, who is the God of the defeated. Ahura Mazda's worshipers are victorious generals and the administrators of a mighty empire. Yahweh's human representatives are, in Haggai's view, a single prophet and the despondent remnant of a still subjected people. The long list of Darius's antagonists was made up of powerful adversaries (see p. 75 above). But there is no sign that Haggai had any desire to incite Zerubbabel, as governor of Judah, to rebel (Bickerman, p. 24, takes another view; cf. also pp. 106f. below on 2:20-23). In short: whereas the Behistun inscription testifies that under Darius, the Persian Empire was stabilized and pacified, and that all the revolts against him were crushed, the prophetic proclamation that Yahweh alone would overthrow all the nations had as its sole purpose the consolation of the disheartened builders of his sanctuary.

In this way God's people are put on to the path of hope. The basis is the prophetic saying about the pathetic beginnings of the temple reconstruction. The people who have become weary and spent over the restoration of Solomon's building are permitted to hope that the future temple will be more beautiful than the first (9a). Material anxieties about the adornment of Yahweh's house are taken quite seriously (see pp. 81 above on כבוד). Something quite unexpected is going to contribute to its "glory" (6-8). But what is ultimately decisive is that in this place Yahweh will confer salvation, peace, and happiness to the full (9b). This prospect consoles the people who have lost heart.

We should note the heightening of the objects of hope. The greater of them (9a) takes on astonishing form. In the light of the amazing messianic fulfillment, the Vulgate arrived at the (philologically wrong) translation (see textual note **7a**): *et veniet Desideratus cunctis gentibus:* "the Desire of all nations shall come" (A. V.). This desire—this "treasure of all nations"—is "the longed-for" Messiah who "shall come." He is "the precious one." By way of patristic and medieval scriptural interpretation, Haggai's saying found an entry into the hymns of the waiting community. ("Come, thou long expected Jesus/. . .Dear desire of ev'ry nation"; "Savior of the nations, come"; "Oh, how shall I receive thee. . .?/ All nations long to see thee"; "The desire of all the nations,/ It is time he should appear.") Cf. G. Krause, *Studien zu Luthers Auslegung der kleinen Propheten,* BHT 33 (1962)

323f.; also his *Aller Heiden Trost* (1957).

Faith marvels at the transformation of the promise in the fulfillment. Faith discovers Jesus: "Behold something greater than Solomon is here" (Matt. 12:42). With the Gospel of John, faith descries "the temple of his body," broken and raised up in three days (John 2:19-22). (On the variableness of God and the alterability of his word, see J. Jeremias, *Die Reue Gottes,* Biblische Studien 65 [1975]; cf. Zech. 8:6; Ps. 77:10.) Beyond all the "shakings" which Israel, the cosmos and the nations experienced then, and experience today, he, "the One desired," will bring about "the unshakable kingdom," in which people are filled with gratitude and eager for service (with Hag. 2:6f., 9 compare Exod. 19:18; Ps. 68:7f.; 77:16-20; 114:7f.; Matt. 24:29; 27:51f.; Heb. 12:26-28). For he will consummate God's gift of salvation, peace and happiness. This promise encourages us, in the earthly rubble and devastation of the community of his people, to play our part in building something new, on the way from "futility" to "glory."

Fourth Scene:
Impurity Is Infectious

Literature

E. Sellin, *Studien zur Entstehungsgeschichte der jüdischen Gemeinde* II (1901). J. W. Rothstein, *Juden und Samaritaner*, BWAT 3 (1908) 5-41. O. Leuze, *Die Satrapieneinteilung in Syrien und im Zweistromland von 520–320*, Schriften der Königsberger Gelehrten Gesellschaft, Geisteswissenschaftliche Klasse 11/4 (1935). J. Begrich, *Die priesterliche Tora*, BZAW 66 (1936) 63-88 = his *Gesammelte Studien*, TB 21 (1964) 232-260. A. Cody, "When Is the Chosen People Called a *gôy*?" VT 14 (1964) 1-7. W. A. M. Beuken, *Haggai—Sacharja 1–8* (1967) 214-216. K. Koch, "Haggais unreines Volk," ZAW 79 (1967) 52-66. G. Fohrer, *Die symbolischen Handlungen der Propheten*, ATANT 25 (1953, 1968[2]). T. N. Townsend, "Additional Comments on Haggai II 10-19," *VT 18* (1968) 559-560. G. J. Botterweck, "גּוֹי": *ThWAT* ed. G. J. Botterweck et al., I (1973) 965-971. A. R. Hulst, "עַם / גּוֹי–Volk": *THAT*, ed. E. Jenni and C. Westermann, II (1976) 290-325. E. M. Myers, "The Use of *tôrâ* in Haggai 2:11 and the Role of the Prophet in the Restoration Community," *The Word of the Lord Shall Go Forth: Fests D. N. Freedman,* ed. C. L. Meyers and M. O'Connor (1983) 69-76 (American Schools of Oriental Research, Special Volume Series, 1). C. Westermann, *Vergleiche und Gleichnisse im Alten und Neuen Testament*, CThM 14 (1984) 75.

Text

2:10 On the twenty-fourth (day) of the ninth (month), in the second year of Darius, the word of Yahweh came to the prophet Haggai, saying,

11 Thus has Yahweh of hosts spoken: Just ask the priests for a directive, saying,

12 If[a] anyone carries holy (sacrificial) flesh in the skirt of his garment, and he touches with his skirt bread[b] or pottage[b] or wine[b] or oil or any kind of food, does it then become holy? The priests answered and said, No.

87

13 Then said Haggai, If, then, one who became unclean by contact with a dead body touches all this, does it then become unclean? The priests answered and said, It does become unclean.

14 Then Haggai began and said,
   So it is with this people,
    so it is with these folk
     in my eyes—saying of Yahweh—
   so is all the work of their hands
    and what they offer there:
    It is unclean.
[a][Because of their morning profits(?). They will suffer pains because of their wickedness.[b] And you [c]"hate in the gates those who reprove."[c]][a]

2:12a הֵן is an Aramaism frequently used for ''if,'' parallel to אִם. It is to be found most often in Job, Ecclesiastes, and Esther.

12b See textual note **2:8b** above.

14a-a MT does not have the additional passage offered by Gk: ἕνεκεν τῶν λημμάτων αὐτῶν τῶν ὀρθρινῶν, ὀδυνηθήσονται ἀπὸ προσώπου πόνων[β] αὐτῶν. καὶ ἐμισεῖτε ἐν πύλαις ἐλέγχοντας.

14b Πόνων may be a corruption within the Greek text of πονηρίων.

14c The last sentence is a reminiscence of Amos 5:10a. The change of person in the three sentences (from ''they'' to ''you'') suggests that this was not a single interpolation, made at one time, but that these were ''successive thrusts'' (W. Rudolph; cf. J. Wellhausen (*Die kleinen Propheten* [1892, 1898³ = 1963⁴] 176 and E. Sellin 464f. As a whole, Gk takes up here classical prophecy's criticism of the cult. See textual note **2:17a-a** above. The rejection of ''this people'' as unclean is explicitly justified by a pointer to culpable behavior.

Form

The limits of the fourth scene are not as clear as those of scene one (1:1-14) and scene three (1:15b—2:9). The beginning is certainly without dispute, because of the chronicler's dating in 2:10 and since the previous promises are completed in 2:9. But in the text as we have it, 2:14 is as problematical, as end of the scene, as is the beginning of scene two in 2:15aα or 1:15a (see pp. 59f. above). The passage 2:15-19 has no apparent connection with 2:10-14, either in style or theme. On the other hand ועתה (''but now'') in 2:15a is comprehensible if it was added later, in order to provide a necessary link (see textual note **2:15a**). At all events, the self-contained character of 2:10-14, both in its formal limits and its theme, is incontrovertible. Cf. also p. 90 below.

    The chronicler's introduction to the new confronting event of God's word (2:10) differs very little from the corresponding phraseology in 1:1, 3, 15a, 15b-2:2. Unlike 1:1 and 1:15b—2:1, the date is given in the order: day—month—year (see p. 35 above), and Darius is not expressly called ''the king,'' as he is in 1:1 and

1:15b. In essentials, we once more find here the language of the Haggai chronicler who uses the formula for introducing the event of God's word (הַיָה דְבַר־יְהוָה אֶל־, "the word of Yahweh came to…," as 1:1, 3; 2:1), and who regularly calls Haggai "the prophet" (as in 1:1, 3; 2:1; see textual note **2:1a** above), in distinction from 1:13; 2:13, 14). Here, in the formula for the event of the word, the phrase used is אֶל ("to") Haggai, not בְּיַד ("through"), as in 1:1, 3; 2:1 (see textual note **2:1a**). But this has a factual reason. For in the immediately following text, Haggai is not the mediator of the word; he is simply its recipient. At the same time, the formula for the event of God's word in 10b clashes uncomfortably with the messenger formula in 11a. This is comprehensible, however, if the Haggai chronicler is taking over the older scene-sketch again, from v. 11 onwards (cf. also 1:1b—2a and pp. 32f. above). That this is the language of the scene-sketch is indicated by the lack of the designation הַנָּבִיא ("the prophet") when Haggai's name is mentioned in 2:13 and 14 (cf. 1:13), although this designation duly appears in v. 10 (cf. on this p. 36 above).

The form of the account in 11-14 in both its parts (11-12 and 13-14) accords with the form of the accounts of prophetic symbolic acts (cf. F. Horst, HAT I/14; G. Fohrer, *Symbolische Handlungen* [1968²], S. Amsler, CAT XIc). In Jeremiah especially, these frequently begin with the messenger formula (cf. 11a with Jer. 13:1; 19:1; 27:2; cf. Hos. 1:2, 4, 6, 9; 3:1; Isa. 8:1; 20:2). This is followed first (1) by the command to perform a particular action (cf. 11b-12a); then (2) by the account of its implementation (cf. 12b-13); and finally (3) by the interpretation of the proceeding (cf. 14). As frequently happens in the accounts of symbolic acts, here too the first two elements are dovetailed, or telescoped, in order to avoid repetition (cf. H. W. Wolff, BK XIV/1, 9, 72 [Eng. *Hosea*, 10f., 58]; G. Fohrer, *Symbolische Handlungen*, 5 et passim). We should expect an account of the implementation of 11b-12a to follow between 12a and 12b, but this is missing; while before v. 13 the issuance of a new commission is lacking too. Both omissions are possible because the correspondence between divine command and prophetic implementation counts as a matter of course. What is most strikingly lacking is an interpretation to follow the first enquiry about the *torah* or instruction (11-12) such as is given in 14 after the second inquiry. The second interpretation could not be emphasized more strongly; it is as if it contained within itself the first interpretation also (see p. 94 below). It carries through the comparison with a triple כֵּן ("so"). Just as the command to put the double question to the priests corresponds, with the messenger formula (11a), to the prophetic charge, so the concluding interpretation in v. 14 is proclaimed as a divine oracle, given through the prophet (נְאֻם־יְהוָה, "saying of Yahweh"). It is within this prophetic framework that the double doctrinal discussion with the priests takes place (12-13). This then forms the basis for the prophetic judgment, taking the place of a symbolic action. The interpretation is simultaneously a prophetic judgment. Thus the scene-sketch introduced by the Haggai chronicler in v. 10 is presented—perfectly rounded off and complete—in 11-14.

Setting

There is no sign that the sentences which follow in 2:15-19 have the same literary location. For it does not emerge that the people condemned (in the third person singular) in v. 14 are identical with those addressed in the second person plural in vv. 15ff.; nor does the subject of uncleanness play any part in the sequel; nor can the beginning of work on the foundations (15-19) be linked in any way with the priestly instruction (11-13). The passage 2:10-14 is only comprehensible if this scene takes place at quite a different time from the scene described in 2:15-19. According to our examination of 1:15a and 2:15ff. (see pp. 60f. above), two to four months elapsed between Haggai's first three appearances on the stage, and this fourth one here. According to 2:10, the middle of December is already past (on December 18, 520, not—as E. J. Bickerman would maintain—December 30, 521; see pp. 74f. above). The pressing question is: what new subject is exercising the minds of Haggai and his listeners, especially since the form of the fourth scene-sketch has become entirely different? On the occasion of Haggai's first appearance, the reporter described, not only the first prophetic sayings, but also their effect (1:12b-13; see p. 34 above); here, on the other hand, he brings out the special preparations the prophet made for what he then says—i.e, his inquiry of the priests, which leads to the prophetic judgment.

With regard to the place meant by "there" (14b), we shall only be able to commit ourselves when we have clarified who "this people" and "this nation" are (v. 14; see p. 94 below). Initially, in the light of the discussion with the priests, we shall have to look for the location of the happening in the temple area in the broadest sense—perhaps near the provisional altar for burnt offerings (cf. Ezra 3:2-6).

Commentary

[2:10]   As far as the cultic calendar goes, the date, the 24th day of the 9th month (= December 18, 520), seems by no means predestined, as it were, for a prophetic utterance—less so, even, than the dates of the first three scenes (but cf. p. 76 above). It is the new event of God's word that determines the new date. At the same time, we shall see that the oracle was this time very probably provoked by a decision which had become necessary because of pressure from outside, a decision which was later recorded in Ezra 4:1-5. At all events, the following verses 11-14 are determined by the process of arriving at a judgment.

[2:11]   This is true for the equipping of the prophet which Yahweh decrees. Haggai has to ask the priests for certain decisions. The priestly decision, or decree, is called תורה, *torah*. Here the word means a type of speech that is as characteristic for the priests as the "counsel" (עֵצָה) for teachers of wisdom and the "(revealed) word" (דָּבָר or חָזוֹן) for the prophets (Jer. 18:18; Ezek. 7:26; Mic. 3:11). The priest was responsible for ritual matters, and had also to distinguish above all between "sacred" and "profane," and between "clean" and "unclean" (Ezek. 44:23); he interpreted (written) edicts orally (Lev. 10:10f.). Instruction of this kind was sought, applied for, or obtained by the laity (Mal. 2:7; Zech. 7:2-4; Deut. 17:9, 11; here the word used is שאל, "entreat"). The obtaining of the *torah* takes the form of a conversation. First of all the case in question is laid before the priest, the exposition coming to a point in a question, which the priest then answers. The layman's question merely permits a choice between two possible answers, and the priest's answer is accordingly simply a straight yes or no.

[2:12] The first case (on הן as conditional particle, "if," cf. textual note **12a**) assumes that someone carries home from a sacrificial meal some meat that has been left over (cf. Jer. 11:15; Lev. 7:19). (Apparently sacrificial meals were possible on the provisionally erected altar, even before the restoration of the temple; cf. Ezra 3:1-6.) The hem of the person's garment was gathered together to form a bag. This permitted only indirect contact with other food.

Food of this general kind is summed up in the collective term "eatables" (מאכל), the term being preceded by the more specific bread, wine, oil, and "something boiled." נזיד, from the root זיד / זוד ("to be hot"), means a meal that is prepared in a cooking pot (סיר הַנָּזִיד 2 Kings 4:39), like Jacob's dish of lentils (Gen. 25:29, 34). The prophet has to ask whether this profane provender becomes holy through contact with "the bag made of the garment" (בכנף, "in the hem" or "skirt" is repeated)—that is, through a merely indirect contact with the holy sacrificial meat (cf. Lev. 6:18-20). The answer is no: indirect contact with what is sacred does not make what is profane holy (for the interpretation see pp. 94f. below).

[2:13] The second case which the prophet lays before the priests (v. 13) is formulated in extremely concentrated form. The phrase טְמֵא־נֶפֶשׁ (טמא = unclean) presupposes that נֶפֶשׁ here means "corpse," which is unusual, but is found in cultic law (Num. 5:2; 6:11; 19:11, 13), where it can be used as an abbreviated term for נֶפֶשׁ מֵת, "dead body" (Lev. 21:11; Num. 6:6). The compound טמא־נפשׁ ("unclean body"), which also occurs in Lev. 22:4, again abbreviates the clearer טָמֵא לָנֶפֶשׁ (Num. 5:2; 9:10), in which the preposition ל introduces the reason for the uncleanness (cf. Gen. 38:24 הָרָה לִזְנוּנִים, "pregnant through harlotry," and BrSynt §107h). The phrase טְמֵא־נֶפֶשׁ accordingly means the person who has become "unclean through a dead body." The question is whether this unclean person would pass on the dead body's uncleanness by touching the articles of food mentioned in v. 12. The priests affirm that this is so. The corpse's uncleanness, which has already communicated itself to the person in contact with it, demonstrates its unusually infecting power, disqualifying food that has been touched by that person from being used for the purposes of worship. Anything that is connected with death has no place in Yahweh's presence (cf. H. W. Wolff, *Anthropologie des Alten Testaments* 43, 159 [Eng. *Anthropology of the Old Testament*, 22, 105]). That is to say, it is unclean. The doctrinal discussion with the

91

priests shows how eminently important it was for ancient Israel to know exactly what was clean and what was unclean in God's eyes, and what powers of infection operated (cf. J. Begrich, *Die priesterliche Tora*, BZAW 66 [1936] 71 = *Gesammelte Studien* [1964] 241). This second case, recorded by a witness, in which a *torah* is obtained from the priests, is the immediate preparation for a final step.

[2:14] In v. 14 the prophet himself raises his voice. Here ענה does not mean "answer," as it does in 12f. The correct translation would be "state" or, more precisely, "begin (to speak)" or "testify." Linking up rather loosely with the second priestly decision, Haggai now proclaims a saying of Yahweh's (αα נאם־ יהוה, "saying of Yahweh"). This saying is therefore undoubtedly prepared for by the priestly *torah*, but it does not take its authority from that. Yahweh himself has empowered his prophet. The triple כן ("so") of the interpretation compares the infecting power of unclean objects with "this people," the decisive, common point of comparison—the third term in which the other two coincide—being the declaration טמא הוא, "it is unclean"). The prophetic oracle therefore goes beyond the priestly instruction in a quite essential way, since the priests had only talked about the technical, cultic effect of contact with various objects by individual laymen in the context of the cult; whereas now the prophet condemns "this people" and "all the work of its hands."

But who is "this people"? In recent years, as earlier, there has been no lack of supporters for the view that this was the same people whom Haggai addresses in 1:4-11; 2:3-9 and 2:15-19* (e.g., P. R. Ackroyd, K. Koch, H. G. May, A. S. van der Woude, and D. L. Petersen; for another view see S. Amsler, 38f.). But for the most part, the arguments put forward by J. W. Rothstein (*Juden und Samaritaner* [1908]) have been substantiated and expanded. In the opinion of this second group of scholars, the people condemned here are "the Samaritans," in a situation similar to that described in Ezra 4:1-5, where "the enemies of Judah and Benjamin" offer their help in building the temple but are rejected by Zerubbabel, Jeshua/Joshua and "the rest of the heads of fathers' houses" (i.e., the heads of families).

The text of Ezra 4:1-5 is seen as historically reliable on the whole, except that the date given in 4:5b is too early. "The substance is historically correct—only the timing is wrong" (O. Leuze, *Satrapieneinteilung* [1935] 41). According to vv. 2f., the incident belongs to the time when the temple was first begun under Zerubbabel. The attempt "to hire counselors" to undermine the building plans (4:5a) fits in with the inspection carried out by the governor Tattenai, according to Ezra 5:3ff. For, under administrative law, Tattenai alone was the superior of the governor of Judah, not the governor of Samaria; see the excursus on the Persian administrative system, p. 39 above.

The rejected Samaritans belonged to the neighboring province of Samaria. It was a mixed population, composed of former Yahweh-believers from what had been the Northern Kingdom, and the descendants of new settlers, such as we are told about in 2 Kings 17:24-34. This second group worshiped "other gods," either exclusively, or at least side by side with Yahweh (2 Kings 17:29, 33).

If it was Samaritans belonging to this group that Haggai meant, then his brusque rejection of "the unclean" is understandable. It then also becomes clear that the whole scene is concerned with the problem of alternative decisions. The interpretation is difficult because, in the abbreviated form which the scene takes, the occasion which gave rise to the question and the subject of the decision are not precisely explained. The reporter is interested solely in the process by which the judgment is arrived at, and in the result. And this also makes it clear why "this nation" and "this people" are referred to only in the third person.

How differently Haggai treats his Jerusalem community, with his questions and his direct address (cf. 1:4f., 7f., 9; 2:3, 4, 15, 18a)! What a struggle to overcome their resistance we sense here, and what encouragement he offers (1:7f.; 2:4f.)! The terse but severe and unique rejection judgment in 2:14 is in harmony neither with the assurances and promises of 1:8b, 13; 2:4, 5b, 6-9, nor with the words addressed to Zerubbabel on the same day (2:20-23).

But how are we to interpret the double declaration הָעָם־הַזֶּה—הַגּוֹי הַזֶּה (translated here "this people ... these folk")? The demonstrative pronouns point to the people who are under discussion—that is to say, presumably to parts of the population who were living in the province of Samaria. Whether Haggai was asked for his judgment as prophet about their proposed cooperation, or whether he gave his opinion unasked, does not emerge. What is intended by the parallel designations הַגּוֹי—הָעָם? Is this no more than a solemn, rhetorical reiteration, pinpointing the same group of people? The two substantives are certainly not infrequently used as synonyms, even though עַם usually tends to imply a reminder of a people's common ancestry and inner kinship, while גּוֹי applies rather to the nation, in the political and territorial sense (cf. G. J. Botterweck, *ThWAT* I; A. R. Hulst, *THAT* II). It is improbable that for Haggai the two words had precisely the same meaning and connotation, if only because he (and the author of the scene-sketch) otherwise, and with considerable consistency, uses עַם only for the community he is directly addressing (1:2, 12b, 13; 2:4), and keeps גּוֹי[ם] for the foreign nations (2:7aα, β, 22). (The Haggai chronicler also uses עַם in talking about שְׁאֵרִית הָעָם, "the remnant of the people"; 1:12a, 14; 2:2.) Will it therefore be permissible to deduce with W. Rudolph (KAT XIII/4, 49f.) that, when he is talking about הָעָם־הַזֶּה, Haggai is thinking of the descendants of the former inhabitants of the Northern Kingdom, whereas with הַגּוֹי הַזֶּה he is referring to the foreign peoples brought in as settlers by the Assyrians? Remarkably enough, 2 Kings 17 never talks about עַם at all, but only about גּוֹי[ם]; the Israelites had put themselves on a level with them (17:8, 11, 15, 26, 29, 33, 41). In Haggai's day too, Israel probably carefully observed the fine distinction in the nuances of the two terms. We find these clearly in Exod. 33:12f., for example, where Moses says to Yahweh, "Consider too that this nation is thy people" (עַמְּךָ הַגּוֹי הַזֶּה). The request means that Yahweh should revise his own attitude, and should cease to treat this גּוֹי as גּוֹי, but should view it as his עַם. Here Haggai may be correcting himself in the opposite sense: this עַם is actually a גוי, cut off from Yahweh. So the word גוי, with its perjorative connotation, may here also contain an echo of the adverse judgment טמא ("unclean").

This judgment applies to "all the work of their hands"—that is to say, also to the people who are offered, or desired, as coworkers in the rebuilding of the temple. It even includes the sacrifices that they offer "there" (on the provisional altar for burnt offerings, according to Ezra 3:2f., see p. 90 above and T. A. Busink, *Der Tempel* [1980] 777f.), in the framework of negotiations with Zerubbabel, Jeshua/Joshua and the other spokesmen of the community of homecomers. קרב *hiphil* is the comprehensive term for the offering of sacrifices. It occurs 25 times in Lev. 1:2—Num. 31:50 alone; cf. R. Rendtorff, *Leviticus,* BK III (1985) 25. Gk: καὶ ὃς ἐὰν ἐγγίσῃ ἐκεῖ, "and whoever approaches there," misunderstands 14b, as if the reading were קרב *qal* instead of *hiphil.*

They are unclean "before me" is the "saying of Yahweh." With this reference to nation and people, the prophetic word goes beyond everything written in the cultic laws about uncleanness. But Yahweh points the prophet in this direction by way of the priests' decision. The Samaritans, who are living in contradiction of the First Commandment, are an acute danger if the people come into contact with them in the course of their common work on the sanctuary. They could seduce to apostasy even the people who are faithful to Yahweh; cf. H. J. Hermisson, *Sprache und Ritus im altisraelitischen Kult,* WMANT 19 (1965) 94f.

The declaratory formula טמא הוא, "it is unclean" (cf. R. Rendtorff, *Die Gesetze in der Priesterschrift,* FRLANT 62 [1954] 74-76) is a judgment that has the force of law in a question of vital importance to the assailed community, which knows that it can of its own strength hardly meet the demands posed by the building of the temple (cf. 2:3ff.). Outside the books of Leviticus and Numbers, this declaratory formula is found only here in the whole of the Old Testament (without the otherwise frequent additional לכם, "to you," found in Lev. 11:4-8, 26f., 38; cf. K. Elliger, *Leviticus,* HAT I/4 150f.).

The judgment that the Samaritans are unclean is the prophetic interpretation of the priestly response to the second *torah* question (v. 13). But what about the first question (v. 12), which is not explicitly interpreted at all? When the priests say that the holy cannot be passed on through indirect contact, what does this mean, in the prophetic view, for the relationship to the Samaritans? It may perhaps mean: do not think that the Samaritans become "holy" just because of their indirect contact with the Jerusalem community of homecomers (by way of cooperation in the temple-building). What is certain, however, is that the community of homecomers will, through the Samaritans, become "unclean." It may be along these lines that the first *torah* prepares for the second, according to the prophetic interpretation.

Purpose and Thrust

On December 18, 520, two months after Haggai's previous appearance (on October 17; see p. 90 above), the community engaged in building the temple found itself faced with a new problem. The rebuilding that had begun three months previously (on September 21) had excited attention far beyond the confines of those who had returned from exile, and the devout, old established Judaeans. Various motives will have prompted the interest of the mixed Samaritan population. Old established Israelites from what had been the Northern Kingdom may well have honestly desired to participate (Ezra 4:2). But in the Samaritan upper classes, on the other hand, suspicion and anxiety will have been roused by Jerusalem's pre-eminent position compared with Samaria (Ezra 5:3f.). As far as the people of Jerusalem were concerned, the huge task (2:3) may well have inspired the wish for Samaritan support.

In this situation the prophetic oracle, with its priestly justification, fell like a thunderbolt. The desire for a coalition could not have been more unequivocally rejected. The people who have been saved and brought home from exile are now to trust in Yahweh's sustaining aid, and in no other help (1:13; 2:4b, 5b). The stringency of the priestly and cultic demarcations between what is ''clean'' and what is ''unclean'' is to mark the uninfringeable limits of the building community as well.

''For modern ears the decision sounds hard. Many people would feel happier if the prophet had made the opposite decision. And yet it is surely not difficult to see that Haggai was merely remaining true to the First and Second commandments of the Decalog, and that he was taking his stand on a separation which Elijah, or Deuteronomy, had also fought for, and won, in their day. For faith in Yahweh was, quite simply, not a religion to which anyone could adhere at will, perhaps even retaining other cultic ties at the same time. This faith had its roots in a divine act of election, and it remained bound to a quite particular national group, or entity. So we should rather see Haggai's importance as being the very fact that—at a time when this fence against the outside world had weakened (though it was a fence for which in former times Israel's finest spirits had fought)—he, like another Elijah, saw at this point an either-or where other people had ceased to see it. Again we have to say that had he decided differently, he would have revoked Isaiah's whole struggle against the policy of alliances; for Isaiah wanted to see Yahweh's relationship to Zion set apart from all pragmatic political practices and their standards. Neither for Isaiah nor for Haggai was this a matter of a ''spiritual'' or religious decision. What they desired was to keep a quite specific historical space free for Yahweh's saving acts'' (G. von Rad, *Theologie des Alten Testament* II [1968⁵] 293f. [cf. Eng. *Old Testament Theology* II, 1965, p. 283]).[1]

The people of Jesus Christ, who are to be ''built into a spiritual house,'' must face the challenge of Haggai's question, whether, and where, they have to watch for the limits of cooperation, and where they must keep a space free for the saving acts of their God (cf. 1 Peter 2:1-10).

The prophetic definition of limits, to which Haggai was led in the context of cooperation in the building of the temple, also had consequences for the structure and editing of the book of Haggai. At all events, it is only in the light of the decision reached in scene four that I am able to understand certain tensions in the transmission of the first three scenes (1:1—2:9; 2:15-19). The special concern of the Haggai chronicler (as distinct from the first scene-sketches) becomes comprehensible in the light of the decision taken in 2:(11-)14.

---

[1] This passage and other, briefer quotations from the same book have been translated directly from the German edition (trans.).

1. Haggai and the author of the scene-sketches had talked in general about the community who were concerned in the building (the people whom Haggai himself addresses) as "the people" (העם; 1:12b, 13; cf. 1:2); in 2:4 the phrase is even כל־עם הארץ, "the entire people of the land" (see p. 73 above). The Haggai chronicler gives a closer definition of these people—the addressees of Haggai's appeal—by talking consistently only about the שארית העם ("the remnant of the people") under Zerubbabel and Joshua (1:12a, 14; 2:2). That is to say, this was the community of those who had returned home from exile; see pp. 51f. above. By limiting the building community so unequivocally, he was taking account of the priestly and prophetic judgment given in 2:14. In so doing he also avoided the misunderstanding to which the phrase כל־עם הארץ ("the entire people of the land") came to be subject in the course of time (cf. 2:4 with Ezra 4:4).

2. The shifting of the second scene (2:15-19), so as to make it *follow* the decision of 2:14, becomes objectively understandable in the light of its content. The editorial "now" in 2:15a signifies that it is only when clear limits have been drawn round the community that the building (2:15) can begin—the building which will be followed, hotfoot, by Yahweh's blessing (2:15, 18a, 19b). Because this was so important to the Haggai chronicler, he cut away 2:15-19 from 1:15a, putting it, with an emphatic ועתה ("but now") after 2:14. The judgment of 2:14 was his legitimation. The "unclean" people would spoil the blessing promised to the restored temple. Cf. p. 63 above.

Haggai 2:20-23

Fifth Scene:
Yahweh's Signet Ring

Literature

W. Böhme, "Zu Maleachi und Haggai," *ZAW* 7 (1887) 210-217 (esp. 215f.). J. W. Rothstein, *Juden und Samaritaner,* BWAT 3 (1908) 42-52. A. Bentzen, "Quelques remarques sur le mouvement messianique parmi les Juifs aux environs de l'an 520 avant J.-Chr," *RHPhR* 10 (1930) 493-503. E. Jenni, *Die politischen Voraussagen der Propheten,* ATANT 29 (1956) 103f. K. Baltzer, "Das Ende des Staates Juda und die Messias-Frage," *Studien zur Theologie der alttestamentlichen Überlieferungen,* ed. R. Rendtorff and K. Koch (1961) 33-43. G. Sauer, *Serubbabel in der Sicht Haggais und Sacharjas,* BZAW 105 (1967) 199-207. K. M. Beyse, *Serubbabel und die Königserwartungen der Propheten Haggai und Sacharja: Eine historische und traditionsgeschichtliche Untersuchung:* AzTh I/48 (1972) 52-58. K. Seybold, "Die Königserwartung bei den Propheten Haggai und Sacharja," *Judaica* 28 (1972) 69-78. T. A. Busink, *Der Tempel von Jerusalem von Salomo bis Herodes II.* (1980) 794-800. E. J. Bickerman, "La seconde année de Darius," *RB* 88 (1981) 23-28.

Text

2:20 Then Yahweh's word came a second time to Haggai on the twenty-fourth (day) of the month, saying:

21 Speak to Zerubbabel,[a] the governor of Judah, saying:
I shake heaven and earth.[b]

22   I overthrow [a]the thrones of kingdoms[a]
         and annihilate the power [of the kingdoms][b] of the nations.
    I destroy the chariots and their riders.
    [c][And I overthrow all their power,
    tear down their frontiers
    and let my chosen one come to strength].[c]
         Horses and riders fall,

97

each one through the sword of his brother.

23 On that day is the saying of Yahweh of hosts:
   I lay hold of you, Zerubbabel—son of Shealtiel—
   my servant,[a] is Yahweh's saying,
   and make you like a signet ring,
   for I have chosen you
      —saying of Yahweh of hosts.

21a Gk supplements on the model of 1:1, 12; 2:2 τὸν τοῦ Σαλαθιηλ, "the son of Shaltiel."

21b Gk expands on the model of 2:6bβ, καὶ τὴν θάλασσαν καὶ τὴν ξηράν, "sea and dry land:"

22a-a Gk θρόνους βασιλέων, "thrones of kings," interprets correctly according to Ges.-K §124r; see p. 103 below.

22b The second ממלכות ("kingdoms") should be omitted. Gk supports MT, but here too, as in aα, presupposes (מ)מלכי ("kings") instead of ממלכות ("of kingdoms"). Both disturb the rhythmical regularity of the three stress cola, spoiling in an unlovely way the rule of alternation which in aα //β properly belongs to the *parallelismus membrorum;* but cf. 2:7a.

22c-c Gk^A adds after 22bα and before 22bβ, καὶ καταστρέψω πᾶσαν τὴν δύναμιν αὐτῶν καὶ καταβαλῶ τὰ ὅρια αὐτῶν καὶ ἐνισχύσω τοὺς ἐκλεκτούς μου ("And I will overthrow their whole power and pull down their frontiers and strengthen my chosen one"). MT has no corresponding passage.

23a עבדי, "my servant," still belongs to the vocative of the person addressed, as apposition, not to the assurance אקח ("I will seize"). For "to take someone as servant," the construction would have to be לקח with acc. and ל; cf. 2 Kings 4:1b; Job 41:4b.

Form

This passage reports Haggai's second appearance on the stage on the 24th day of the 9th month = December 18, 520. After introducing the confronting event of God's word, it brings two prophetic oracles (21b-22 and 23), which are loosely joined by way of the link formula in 23aα ביום ההוא, "on that day." In terms of form criticism, however, the two sayings differ considerably.

   The introduction (20-21a), with the elements of which it is composed—formula for the confronting event of God's word, date, and addressee—is clearly reminiscent of the corresponding accounts of the event of the word earlier in the book (cf. 1:1; 1:15a,b—2:2; 2:10). Only the number of the day is given here; but this was already the case in 1:15a, where the month and the year were already known. Here it is easily understandable, since the day—uniquely in Haggai—is explicitly that of the previous oracle (שנית, "a second time," 2:10). Zerubbabel is introduced in 21a as recipient of the oracle with אל ("to"). This corresponds to 2:2 and also to 1:1. But that in 20a Haggai as mediator of Yahweh's word, should also be introduced with אל is in accord neither with 1:1, 3 nor with 2:1, where the preposition used for the mediator of the word is ביד ("through"). אל־חגי ("to Haggai")

98

in 2:20 has probably been taken over without reflection from 2:10, unless indeed 2:20-21α is the work of a different author (see p. 36 above and W. Böhme, *ZAW* 7 [1887] 215f.). In 2:10 אל is correct, since it designates Haggai as the receiver of the word. The only other irregularities in 20-21a are that the formula for the event of the word stands at the beginning; that the name Haggai is not accompanied by the description הנביא ("the prophet"; see otherwise 1:1, 3, 12a; 2:1, 10); and that in 2:21 "Zerubbabel, the governor of Judah" is not flanked by his father's name (see in contrast 1:1, 12a, 14; 2:2, 23). In 2:23 the oracle link-formula "on that day" appears for the first and only time in Haggai. All in all, the points of agreement with the other accounts of the confronting event of the word have more weight than the differences, all of which can be explained on factual grounds. We may therefore again see the Haggai chronicler at work as editor, or redactor, in 2:20-21a and in the oracle link-formula in 2:23aα.

With 21b-23 he takes over for the last time the scene-sketch of one of the prophet's disciples or pupils, with two prophetic oracles. One interesting point is that, although in 21a the Haggai chronicler introduces Zerubbabel as "governor of Judah" (which is in line with his usual practice; cf. 1:1, 14; 2:2), Haggai himself, according to the scene-sketch, leaves out the official Persian title (23aα). Both cases conform to our findings with regard to 2:2 and 4; on 1:2, see p. 51 above.

In terms of form criticism, the first of the two oracles must be described as a theophany announcement, with its consequences, in line with the traditions of the holy war (cf. 2:6f.; also pp. 80f. above and p. 102 below); whereas the second must be seen as an appointment or designation, in accord with court traditions.

Looking at them in more detail, we can detect three additional differences in the form of the two sayings.

1. Only the second is explicitly addressed to Zerubbabel, although the announcements in the first saying are also directed to him, according to 21a.

2. Only the first, with its parallel units, displays a rhythmical structure. Verses 21b-22 are most readily to be seen as two three-stress tricola (to which Gk seems to add a third), if we also read 21b as having three stresses and excise ממלכות ("of kingdoms") in 22aβ as a secondary addition (see textual note **22b**). The second saying, on the other hand, in the form in which we have it, must be read as prose. Yet here above all we should also expect the poetic structure associated with oral delivery; and this can in fact be restored if the stereotyped link-formula ביום ההוא ("on that day") and the twice repeated נאם יהוה צבאות ("saying of Yahweh of hosts") in aα[1] and bβ as well as בן־שאלתיאל ("son of Shealtiel") in aα are all viewed as written interpolations to the scene-sketch. The structure that then clearly emerges is that of two two-stress bicola:

עבדי נאם־יהוה   אקחך זרבבל
כי־בך בחרתי   ושמתיך כחותם

From the broad, rolling periods of the three-stress tricola in 21b-22, which proclaim the revolution in world events, the prophetic utterance builds up to the solemnly terse verses of the call to Zerubbabel, in which every beat is stressed.

3. It is strange that the present text of 23 includes, not only a נאם־יהוה

("saying of Yahweh"; aα²) but also a twice-repeated נאם יהוה צבאות ("saying of Yahweh of hosts"; aα¹ and bβ), whereas in the first saying neither of the two oracle formulas appears, even though here too Yahweh's own first-person address ("I") is dominant (21b-22bα). But this disproportion is less crass if only the briefer text of 23, which I have proposed above, belonged to the oracle proclamation.

Excursus: (צבאות) נאם יהוה *in the Book of Haggai*

The divine saying formula (saying of Yahweh [Sebaoth]) occurs unusually often in the little book of Haggai. We need only make a comparison: נאם ("saying") occurs in the whole of the Old Testament 376 times (according to H. Eising, *ThWAT* V, 120). Of these instances, 4 are found in Hosea, 2 in Micah; whereas in only two chapters in the book of Haggai we find it 12 times, 6 of them in the short form נאם יהוה, "saying of Yahweh" (to which we shall assign the symbol S in this discussion), and 6 of them in the longer form נאם יהוה צבאות, "saying of Yahweh Sebaoth" (which we shall call L). If we take 2:23 as our starting pointz, S following עבדי ("my servant") is probably the original reading, whereas the twice-repeated L is probably a later interpolation (see above, the previous paragraph). In all three instances, the formula has the function of stressing an immediately proximate "I," as Yahweh's own "I": "*My* servant—saying of Yahweh"; "Saying of Yahweh Sebaoth—*I* lay hold of you"; "You *I* choose—saying of Yahweh Sebaoth." This function—to stress Yahweh's "I"—can also be detected in 2:14 ("before *me*—saying of Yahweh"), as well as in 1:9, 13; 2:8, 9b, 17, and also in 2:4bβ. The exception is the double occurrence of the encouraging call in 2:4a. When the formula occurs 3 times in 2:4, we may deduce (comparing the verse with 2:23) that S and L have a different provenance. In 2:23 it emerged that probably only S derives from Haggai himself (in his oral proclamation), whereas L is a written addition. The same may well apply to 2:4, where S seems an almost indispensable element in the call to Zerubbabel and the people. In 2:14 also, S is probably Haggai's own utterance. The question of provenance is most uncertain in 1:9 and 2:17. The fact that in 2:4a, in the call to the high priest (which was only added by the Haggai chronicler; see p. 73 above), both S and L are missing, suggests that neither of the formulas originally derives from the Haggai chronicler, but that as a rule they either go back to Haggai himself (especially S) or (especially L) derive from the author of the scene-sketches. Since both formulas stress Yahweh's "I" in each given case, their main function in the proclamation is to strengthen the assailed. This is clearly true of S in 2:4 (in view of the substance of 2:3) and of 2:14 (with reference to "this people," the Samaritans). In liking to interpolate L, Haggai's disciple points through his "Yahweh Sebaoth" to the almighty Lord (Gk: κύριος παντοκράτωρ, *kyrios pantocrator*), who is the Lord of all armies as well; for it is these armies that are under discussion in the context, to a more or less obvious degree; compare two occurrences of L in 2:23 with 2:22 and 2:8, 9b with 2:6f.

Setting

The interpretation of the two prophetic oracles will have to take into consideration their literary setting. What significance does it have when Yahweh's theophany among the nations and Zerubbabel's appointment, or designation, are proclaimed and recorded on the same day as the decision about "this people"? Cf. 2:20-21a with 2:10 and 2:14. Are the two political decisions equally explosive? To this we must add the pressing question: what is the relationship between the highly up-to-the-minute decisions of this momentous day and the prophetic utterances about the building of the temple in the previous three scenes?

Are these last sayings addressed to the same general public? Or was Zerubbabel's designation, at least (v. 23), announced to a more intimate or restricted group? Was it perhaps even deliberately kept secret? Cf. 1 Sam. 10:1; 16:13; 1 Kings 11:29; 2 Kings 9:6; also p. 102 below.

The solution of problems of this kind is linked with the question, how far was Haggai's proclamation dependent on that particular hour in world history? Like most other scholars, we have assumed that the 24th day of the 9th month in the 2nd year of Darius I's reign was the equivalent of December 18, 520 (contrary to the dating of E. J. Bickermann, who has recently pleaded for December 30, 521; see the excursus: "The Second Year of Darius," pp. 74f. above). It is true that at the later of these two dates the most severe unrest in the Persian Empire which followed Cambyses' death had largely been surmounted (see p. 75 above). But prophetic confidence in Yahweh's purposes in history was too deeply rooted in the traditions of Israel's faith for this to have been at the mercy of any short-term ebb and flow in the world of the nations. This being so, even in December 520 Haggai too may well have taken over from political events in the world of 522–521 features and colorings which helped him to bring out more strongly the picture of Yahweh's future interventions.

Commentary

[2:20] Elsewhere also we find two different prophetic utterances recorded for the same day (שֵׁנִית, "a second"): in 2 Sam. 7:3 and 4ff. and in Jer. 28:5-9 and 12-16. In these other passages the first saying in each case is a personal verdict on the part of Nathan and Jeremiah respectively; it is only the second saying that claims reception as Yahweh's word. In this second saying Nathan has to proclaim the very opposite of the view he himself had maintained previously. But Jeremiah has to announce a clear confirmation and elucidation of his own reflections. In Haggai's case, the new scene on the same day takes up a fresh theme—unless we prefer to see it as a decisive further development. For the judgment about "this people," with whom there is to be no contact because they are "unclean" (vv. 12-14), is now followed by the announcement of the downfall of the great powers in general (vv. 21b-22), together with a special call to Zerubbabel (v. 23).

[2:21-22] Both sayings in this second scene can be interpreted as a "boost" to the people addressed, after the severe trial of the restriction imposed on them in 2:14. Nothing suggests that Haggai proclaimed the sayings of the 24th day of the 9th month (= December 18) to a wide public, as he did his earlier sayings—either explicitly so (1:2, 12-14; 2:2, 4) or at least quite evidently, as can be deduced from the plural forms of address and the corresponding content and forms of speech (1:4-10; 2:15f., 18a, 19b; 2:3). We find nothing like this in the oracles of 2:14, 21b-23. In 2:23 it is Zerubbabel alone who is expressly addressed. But 2:21b-22 also falls under Yahweh's command to the prophet to speak (only) to Zerubbabel (21a; cf. in contrast 2:2). The prophet's first appearance of the day (vv. 10-14) affects only Haggai himself initially (v. 11). He is led to a prophetic verdict for which no addressee is stated. Nothing tells us that the decision was passed on to a popular assembly. And in fact its substance makes it more probable that the verdict was communicated either to a group of elders (cf. Ezra 5:5; 6:8, 14) or even to Zerubbabel only (in accordance with 21a and 23), as spokesman of the community of homecomers (cf. Ezra 4:3). In either event, the decision was a hard one for the person who had to draw the appropriate conclusions.

The second saying of the day may therefore start from the assumption that Zerubbabel, as leader of the gola community, would have to reckon with political difficulties. Tensions threatened to loom up between Samaria and Jerusalem. The Northern province, whose administrative capital was Samaria, possessed a (semi-) heathen upper class, going back to Assyrian-Babylonian times (2 Kings 17:24-34; see p. 93 above; also Ezra 4:2f.). These people mistrusted the thousand who were forming the new aristocracy in Judah, and who had recently returned home from exile with Zerubbabel and Joshua (see pp. 51f. and 95 above). Between these two groups lived the old established Judaeans and North Israelites, who had had ties with the sanctuary in Jerusalem since time immemorial. The inspection which the satrap from Damascus, Tattenai, carried out in Jerusalem in 519, soon after the temple building had been begun under Zerubbabel, reflects the profound mistrust between the two rival aristocracies; cf. Ezra 5:1-10: also A. Alt, *Kleine Schriften zur Geschichte des Volkes Israels* (1953-59), II, 316, 335; K. M. Beyse, *Serubbabel und die Königserwartung...* (1972) 52ff.; A. H. J. Gunneweg, *Geschichte Israels bis Bar Kochba* (1972) 126. People scented rebellion and attempts at a coup d'état. Suspicion, at the very least, was in the air when Haggai raised his voice a second time on the 24th day of the 9th month (= December 18) and addressed a Zerubbabel who perhaps found himself under attack.

Haggai began with the same words with which he had buoyed up a wider public two months previously (on the 21st day of the 7th month = October 17, 520); cf. 2:6bα with 2:3f. Addressing the governor, he bears witness to the "I" of his God, who calls into the service of his universal rule the cataclysms of heaven and earth—that is to say, the whole cosmos—with their earthquakes, tempests, and floods. And to this universal rule belongs his sanctuary, whose rebuilding he now expects (see pp. 80f. above). Haggai thereby picks up the traditional assurance, but in what he goes on to say he draws on his knowledge of the nations of his own day (22). Motifs from the holy war are touched upon (cf. G. von Rad, *Der heilige Krieg im alten Israel,* ATANT 20 [1951] 65f.; K. Galling, *Studien,* 139f.). But it is difficult to distinguish between what is traditional and what is topical. The catchword introducing Yahweh's announcement in 22a and 22b (והפכתי) is actually proclaimed twice, and in using it Haggai offers the worried Zerubbabel the immediate and lasting reminder that Yahweh is the God who controls all the political conditions and affairs of the great powers. The initial meaning of הפך is, "turn," whether it be cakes (Hos. 7:8; cf. H. W. Wolff, BK XIV/1, 161; Eng.

Hosea [1986⁴] 126), or whether it be the direction of the wind (Exod. 10:19). It then becomes the word characterizing all kinds of overturns and total alterations. It is linked especially with the traditions about Sodom and Gomorrah, where it describes both the destruction of the cities themselves and the devastation of the country; cf. Gen. 19:25, 29; Deut. 29:23; Isa. 13:19; Jer. 20:16; 49:18; Lam. 4:6. But in Haggai—and this is unique in the Old Testament—כסא ממלכות becomes the object of the overthrow. Scholars have tried to interpret the phrase in a singular sense ("throne of kings": K. Elliger; W. Rudolph; S. Amsler), thinking of the central Persian government. But the Septuagint (see textual note **22a-a**) has correctly understood the Hebrew view that when a substantive (*nomen regens*) is linked with a genitive (*nomen rectum*), the pluralizing of the *nomen rectum* is sufficient to indicate a plural sense in the *nomen regens*. Here, therefore, the overthrow of a whole number of thrones of kingdoms is being announced. The view was suggested to contemporaries by the beginning of the reign of Darius I, with its often rebellious and then deposed kings (see pp. 74f. above). The final overthrow of all thrones will be brought about by Yahweh.

The parallel utterance in v. 22aβ declares that what is at issue in the overthrow of the thrones is royal power. חזק means the power of the nations which, in the form of military achievement, leads to warlike intervention and, if at all feasible, to the preeminence of the mighty (Amos 6:13). It is power of this kind that Yahweh is going to destroy. שמד *hiphil* means the extermination which was to be carried out in the context of the sacral prerogatives of the holy wars of the early days; cf. Deut. 2:21f.; 9:3; Josh. 7:12; 11:20 with Amos 2:9; 9:8; Zech. 12:9 and H. W. Wolff, BK XIV/2, 204 (Eng. *Joel and Amos* [1985³], 168). What Yahweh is going to annihilate is not the nations themselves but their militant nature.

This becomes even clearer in 22b, when the strongest and swiftest weapons are given over to destruction: the chariot squadrons; cf. H. Weippert, "Pferd und Streitwagen," *BRL²*, 250-255. Haggai names "chariots" (מרכבה), "horses" (סוסים), and רכבים. The last of these terms designates the team, the riders in the chariot. It was only seldom that the charioteer was alone, for since he held the reins he could only impress the enemy, not fight. (We can see this on an ivory from Megiddo, *BRL²*, 70, Pl. 19,3.) As a rule there was a bowman, as assailant (cf. J. Pritchard, *The Ancient Near East in Pictures* [1954] 172, 183f.), and it was not infrequent for the team to include a shield-bearer as defense. The horses and their team are told here that they will "fall" (ירד, "be cast down," "perish"). Again the Exodus tradition and traditions from the holy war (Exod. 14:25; 15:4, 21; Isa. 34:7; 43:17; Jer. 48:15) merge with experiences from the most recent Persian period (cf. Behistun §§18, 20, 32, 42 and frequently: "mounted troops"). When, in the final clause of the oracle (22bγ), Haggai then says that each man will perish "through the sword of his brother," we are also expected to think of a repetition of the divinely inspired panics of the early Israelite period (Judg. 7:22; cf. Ezek. 38:21; Zech. 14:13), as well as of the act that triggered off Darius I's wars of succession. For fratricide is one of the main themes of the Behistun inscriptions. Cambyses had murdered his brother Smerdis/Bardiya (§10). But this murder was kept secret. "Then lies became rampant in the land." Gaumâta first of all announced that he was Smerdis, Cyrus's son, Cambyses' brother (§11). Later, one rebel after another claimed to be Smerdis (see, for example, §§ 41, 45; also pp. 74f. above). Darius calls them "lying kings." When Haggai takes up the theme of fratricide and the bewildering, divinely inspired terror, he is emphasizing at the end of his oracle that the powerful and the violent will ultimately put an end to one another in their panic. Yahweh will bring about the downfall of all militant warriors, and Zerubbabel's people will not be endangered by their armies in the process. Provided that the saying in 21b-22 is specifically communicated to the governor of Judah (21a), it will relieve him of all fear of political entanglements (following the decision in 2:14).

If we compare 2:21b-22 with 2:6-7, we first of all find points of agreement. Both begin with the announcement of cosmic cataclysms brought about through Yahweh, the wording being identical (6bα = 21b, somewhat expanded in 6bβ). Both pass on to political upheavals in the world of the nations (הגוים, "the nations," in 7a and 22aβ). But here the differences begin. Verse 7aα merely announces briefly, if emphatically, that Yahweh "shakes all nations." Verse 22 can be understood as an elucidation of what this upheaval means, since it talks about the overthrow of national power and the destruction of military potential. Verse 7aβ.b, on the other hand, speaks surprisingly about the arrival of treasures from all the nations that have been so shaken—treasures that are to be used for the adornment of Yahweh's sanctuary, from which the gift of peace will ultimately proceed (9b). In the light of this, it is not surprising if in v. 22 the threat to kingly thrones leads essentially speaking to the annihilation of all evil warlike practices—a promise which indirectly contains a consolation for Zerubbabel. Codex Alexandrinus already adds as goal of the surmounting of all warlike ways of achieving power that Yahweh will "let his chosen one come to strength" (cf. textual note **22c-c**).

[2:23] The Masoretic text only introduces the turn to salvation in v. 23. The text is directly addressed to Zerubbabel. The literary link-phrase "on that day" (cf. H. W. Wolff, BK XIV/2, 373 [Eng., *Joel and Amos,* 324]) dates the fulfillment of the following assurance as being the end of the kingdoms of the world in all their violence (21b-22), which for Haggai does not have to mean a delay in the encouraging imminent expectation of 2:6 (see pp. 80f. above on v. 6aβ). The thrice-used formula for a divine saying (see pp. 99f. above) shows how in this oracle every word has the greatest possible weight—in what it does *not* say as well. Thus Zerubbabel is no longer addressed by the Persian title for the governor of Judah פחת יהודה (as he still is even in 21a). Nor is he solely given his own name. He is now called "son of Shealtiel" (at least in the written scene-sketch; cf. p. 99 above), which indicates his origin, though without touching directly on his Davidic descent (cf. pp. 38ff. above).

The actual oracle itself begins with אקחך ("I will lay hold of you"). The first person singular of the verb לקח, with the second person singular pronominal suffix, shows immediately what may be said of the whole saying: in its direct address it deals exclusively with Yahweh's relationship to Zerubbabel. And in this context לָקַח has a merely limited meaning of its own. In similar contexts the word announces interventions that are going to bring about a change of place, calling, and function (Gen. 24:7; Exod. 6:7; Num. 3:12; Deut. 4:20; Josh. 24:3; 2 Sam. 7:8; 2 Kings 2:3; 14:21; 23:30; Amos 7:15; cf. H. W. Wolff, BK XIV/2, 362 [Eng. *Joel and Amos,* 314]). As if it were an adverb, it characterizes the action that follows as Yahweh's sovereign initiative.

The saying is addressed to "my servant." The word עֶבֶד ("servant") has a wide range of meaning. We need only mention the domestic slave (Gen. 24:2), the soldier (2 Sam. 2:12), the minister (Jer. 36:24), Moses (Deut. 34:5), the Babylonian king Nebuchadnezzar (Jer. 25:9; 27:6), but above all King David. When it is applied to David "Yahweh's servant" (עַבְדִּי, "my servant") positively becomes a title (2 Sam. 7:5, 8; 1 Kings 11:32, 34; Ezek. 34:23f.; 37:24; Ps. 78:70; 89:3; 132:10). Zerubbabel is therefore addressed in the same way as David. But he is not appointed "Yahweh's servant" for the first time here (see textual note **23a**); he is this already. According to Haggai's line of thinking, this relationship will have been related to Zerubbabel's efforts for the building of the temple. In substance, the title of servant points to willing obedience in confidence and faithfulness (Isa. 42:1; Ps. 89:3).

In taking possession of his servant, Yahweh promises him something new. The imperfect אֶקָּחֲךָ (in its adverbial function) is followed by the clinching perfect construction, pointing to the future: וְשַׂמְתִּיךָ. שִׂים with an accusative and כְּ means "make the equivalent of," "make into something" (Gen. 13:16; 1 Kings 19:2; Hos. 2:3). Zerubbabel is therefore now assigned the function of a "seal." In the ancient Near East, חוֹתָם means a seal that is diversely engraved, especially in the form of a roll or cylinder seal, or as scarab; it could be impressed with a picture device and/or an inscription (name); cf. P. Welten, "Siegel und Stempel," *BRL*², 299-307 (with illustrations). It could be worn as an ornament round the neck ("laid on the heart"), or on the arm (Song of Sol. 8:6), or as a ring on one of the fingers of the right hand (Gen. 41:42; Esther 3:10; Jer. 22:24). The term could therefore be used as a metaphor for particular beauty (Ezek. 28:12, with the comment by W. Zimmerli, BK XIII, 683 [Eng. *Ezekiel,* 1979]). Thus H. Ewald (*Propheten des Alten Bundes* III [1868²] 186) reads our text in the light of Song of Sol. 8:6, interpreting it as meaning "take you and keep you as the signet ring—that is, cherish you as the most precious jewel."

Essentially, however, the seal served to authenticate legal enactments, identify property, and authorize a proxy. Thus the seal is a legally valid equivalent for a signature on documents (Jer. 32:10-44; 1 Kings 21:8). To give someone else one's own seal meant conferring on him legal authority and entire trust. What this promise is really saying is that Yahweh will make Zerubbabel a seal in this sense. There is only a single comparable text in the Old Testament: Jer. 22:24. There, in the prophetic word, Yahweh makes his rejection of King Jehoiachin unequivocally clear by threatening to do the most preposterous thing: to tear off the signet ring from his finger—that is, to throw away the most precious token of his identity.

Jehoiachin was released from his prison in exile in the 55th year of his life (2 Kings 24:8; 25:27). Since Zerubbabel was born in exile (see p. 38 above), he may very well have known his grandfather. Did he, or did Haggai, know Jeremiah's word of judgment addressed to his grandfather? And was he therefore also familiar with the otherwise unknown metaphor of the signet ring? This is certainly true of Sir. 49:11f., where Zerubbabel is praised as being "like a signet on the right hand," the wording therefore combining Jer. 22:24 with Hag. 2:23. Does Haggai mean to tell Zerubbabel that through him Yahweh is going to give the rejected Davidic dynasty a fresh continuation? (Cf. 2 Sam. 7:16 and S. Mowinckel, *He that Cometh* [1956] 119; K. M. Beyse, *Serubbabel und die Königserwartungen ...*, 59.) In Haggai the context does not suggest a reminiscence of the Nathan prophecy. Do we not have to relate the saying about the seal to the preceding scene? A seal authenticates a piece of legal business and has a binding effect. To seal something also includes an element of completion. Zerubbabel, as Yahweh's seal, would then be the guarantor of the temple's completion. In this respect the assurance would be a consolation to the people who were downhearted, corresponding to Zech. 4:9. In addition, Yahweh's seal would guarantee the fulfillment of the promises associated with the building of the temple. Thus v. 22 is an encouragement to the people who had been made anxious by the decision of 2:14.

Let us first of all bear in mind that the assurance that Zerubbabel is going to be the equivalent of a seal is the really new and important thing stated in this oracle; for the כי ("because") clause, with its verifying or assertative perfect tense, which follows the saying about the seal, does not develop this statement in any real sense; it names the already-given reason for what Yahweh is going to do: "I have chosen you." בחר, "choose," often approaches אהב ("love") in meaning; e.g., Deut. 4:37; Isa. 41:8. In this clause of reason too, which adheres to the direct address, what is under discussion is Yahweh's personal relationship to Zerubbabel (just as it is in אקחך, עבדי, and ושמתיך). And with בחר, as with עבדי ("my servant"), a note is sounded which is frequent in the Davidic traditions: 1 Sam. 16:8-10; 2 Sam. 6:21; 1 Kings 8:16; 11:34; Ps. 78:70; 1 Chron. 28:4. It is perhaps significant that Ps. 78:70 includes all the keywords of our Haggai saying: "lay hold of," לקח; "my servant," עבדי; "choose," בחר. Only the image of the seal, and hence the really new feature, is lacking in the psalm verse. But Ps. 78:70 mentions David, whereas the name is missing in Haggai. So it is not entirely improbable that, when the saying announces that Zerubbabel will be the equivalent of a seal, this means that he will in the future be declared the new David. But it must be stressed that this promise is couched in extremely muted terms. Important words and themes belonging to the messianic expectation are missing—not only the name of David, but also words such as "anoint" (משח) and "king" (מלך). More important still: nothing is said about the struggle, the victory, and the peace of the Messiah (Isa. 9:6f.; Zech. 9:9f.; cf. Ps. 2:9, 12; 110:5f.). Has this theme been wound up with the announcement that Yahweh will overthrow the great powers (v. 22)? Is what is to be sealed "on that day" through Zerubbabel just this—the fact that Yahweh has prepared an end to the wars of those great powers? It is not so much as suggested that particular acts are left to Zerubbabel in the world of the nations and among his own people. There is no indication that he is to administer the peace—still less that subversive actions against Darius's empire might be expected of him (though for a different view see E. J. Bickermann, *RB* 88 [1981], 24f. and p. 75 above; also T. A. Busink, *Tempel* [1980], 799).

The promise applies solely to the friendly, intimate "I–Thou" relationship between Yahweh and Zerubbabel: "I will lay hold of *thee*," "*my* servant," thus "I will make *thee* a signet ring." We have seen that the essentially new feature is the saying about the seal. But the question is: when the servant is called a seal, what function does this give him? The obedient servant becomes the one on whom authority has been conferred; the one who serves becomes the representative; the familiar friend becomes the guarantor. It is an open linguistic question whether this new definition of the relationship to God should be considered as carrying with it messianic features; cf. K. M. Beyse, *Serubbabel und die Königserwartungen ...*, 9, 41. But what is at all events characteristic is that here a messiah is not *proclaimed* (as for example in Zech. 9:9f.), but that Zerubbabel is *addressed*. The man spoken to is the initiator of the temple building, the man who was obedient to Haggai's word and who concerned himself with the place of Yahweh's presence, Yahweh's blessing, and Yahweh's peace. It is this man who can see himself appointed Yahweh's most precious jewel—and even as his authorized governor, indeed, as "seal," that is to say, the guarantor that the temple will be completed and the divine promises fulfilled. He too is still living in an hour of waiting, in the time of small beginnings. But as he waits he has no longer to be afraid of hostility. Yahweh's hand already has him in its grasp.

Purpose and Thrust

Zerubbabel had need of this assurance. Why did Haggai retreat into silence, after a bare four months of goading initiative? Did he die soon after his last oracle? Or did Zerubbabel die? Was he recalled as governor by the central government? Did he end up on the scaffold as a rebel? Or in prison in Susa? Or in hiding in some mountain cranny in Syria? (Cf. T.A. Busink, *Tempel*, 799.) Scholars' questions are as inquisitorial as were Tattenai's long ago, according to Ezra 5:3ff. Neither Haggai nor Ezra answers them. Nothing gives us sufficient reason for accusing Zerubbabel of short-sighted enthusiasm, as if he had put himself at the head of an unrealistically impetuous movement for liberty. The sayings in vv. 22 and 23 do not permit any such conclusion. And according to 2:4, he was, if anything, on the fainthearted side. Later, in the account of the completion of the temple in Ezra 6:14ff., he is not so much as mentioned—in spite of Zech. 4:9. For Haggai, and hence, up to now, for any soundly based Zerubbabel research, the story of this governor of Judah ends with the two divine sayings in 2:21b-22 and 23. After that, darkness descends. Even the two passages Zech. 4:6-10 and 6:12f. do not take us any further.

Yet in spite of all the gloomy speculations, the last saying we read in Haggai contains not a single hopeless word, and not a syllable of disappointment.

On the contrary, the only sentences addressed to Zerubbabel clearly call him to become the bearer of hope. As governor of Judah he was undoubtedly familiar with conditions in the Persian empire, including the unrest that followed Gaumâta's revolt and Cambyses' death (see pp. 75f. above). So he was surely able to see Haggai's individual, willful interpretation of the expectation of peace in 21b-22 (cf. 2:6-9) for what it was: not as an appeal for any kind of warlike leadership or participation, but as Yahweh's disempowerment of all the powerful, as his annihilation of all instruments of destruction, as the self-laceration of all aggressors. The governor of Judah was no warrior.

Verse 23 designates him as the personal bearer of hope. This saying is loosely linked with the preceding passage, as a kind of coda. If we see it as associated in content with 21b-22, then Zerubbabel is promised that at the end of all the discord in the world he will be Yahweh's seal, the seal with which he endorses the completion of peace dependably, effectively, bindingly. Perhaps we may also relate this personal word to Zerubbabel's life's work—the building of the temple—and to the promises which Haggai associated with that (cf. 1:8b; 2:9b: 2:19b). In spite of all the obscurities of history Zerubbabel remains an enduring image: he is the bearer of hope, in accordance with the promise of his God which he received.

What happened to Zerubbabel is a riddle. What is not a riddle is that here we have a person who was drawn into a unique bond with the God of Israel. Why this particular Persian governor and son of David should have been made God's "seal" is a riddle. What is not a riddle is that according to this saying, God's free, loving election alone was the reason for his calling. The number of witnesses in the Old Testament who were called and failed is a riddle (cf. R. P. Carroll, *When Prophecy Failed* [1979] 157-168). But what is a fact is that their word nonetheless called into being new hope for fulfillment. At the end of the long succession of Old Testament witnesses, God's house on earth and peace in the world find their dependable verification in the Servant of God, Jesus. It is from this that the Christian faith lives, on its way through all the tremors and the shocks, to the kingdom "that cannot be shaken"; cf. 2:6f., 21f. with Heb. 12:26-28.

Manuscript Sigla

A	Codex Alexandrinus, LXX
α′	Aquila's Greek version of the OT
Arm	The Armenian version
B	Codex Vaticanus, LXX
Bo	The Bohairic version
Gk^A	Code Alexandrinus
Gk^B	Codex Vaticanus 75
Gk (or LXX)	The Septuagint (Greek version of the OT)
Gk^L (or L)	Lucian's recension of LXX
Gk^R	Codex Veronensis, LXX
MT	The Masoretic text of the Hebrew Bible
S	Codex Sinaiticus, LXX
σ′ (or Symm)	Symmachus's Greek version of the OT
Sy^h	Syriac version of Origen's Hexapla
Syr (or S)	The Syriac version (Peshitta)
T (or Targ)	Targum or Targums
θ′	Theodotion's Greek version of the OT
Vg	The Vulgate

A more complete list of sigla may be found in *Biblia Hebraica Stuttgartensia,* ed. K. Elliger and W. Rudolph (Stuttgart: Deutsche Bibelgesell-schaft, 1977), pp. xliv-xlviii.

Hebrew Grammars Cited

Bauer-Leander   H. Bauer and P. Leander, *Historische Grammatik der Hebräischen Sprache des alten Testaments* I, Halle 1922.

BrSynt   C. Brockelmann, *Hebräische Syntax*, Neukirchen 1956.

Joüon   Paul Joüon, *Grammaire de l'Hébreu Biblique*, Rome: Institut Biblique Pontifical, 1947^2.

Ges.-K   *[F. H. W.] Gesenius' Hebrew Grammar, 2nd English edition revised in accordance with the 28th German ed. (1909) by A. E. Cowley*, Oxford 1910, reissued 1946.

Abbreviations

ABR	*Australian Biblical Review*
AfO	*Archiv für Orientforschung*
AION	*Annali dell'Istituto Universitario Orientale di Napoli*
AJA	*American Journal of Archeology*
AJSLL	*American Journal of Semitic Languages and Literature*
ANET	*Ancient Near Eastern Texts Relating to the Old Testament*, ed. J. Pritchard
AOAT	*Alter Orient und Altes Testament*
AOT	Altorientalische Texte zum Alten Testament
ArPap	*Aramaic Papyri of the Fifth Century B.C.*, ed. A. Cowley
ASTI	*Annual of the Swedish Theological Institute* (in Jerusalem)
ATANT	Abhandlungen zur Theologie des Alten und Neuen Testaments
ATD	Das Alte Testament Deutsch
AuS	G. Dalman, *Arbeit und Sitte in Palästina*, 6 vols. (1928–1942)
AzTh	Arbeiten zur Theologie
BA	*Biblical Archeologist*
BASOR	*Bulletin of the American Schools of Oriental Research*
BC	Biblischer Commentar
BeO	*Bibbia e Oriente*
BHH	*Biblisch-historisches Handwörterbuch*
BHT	Beiträge zur historischen Theologie (Tübingen, 1929ff.)
Bibl	*Biblica*
BiblStud	Biblische Studien (Neukirchen)
BibOr	*Biblica et Orientalia*
BiKi	*Bibel und Kirche*
BiViChr	*Bible et Vie Chrétienne*
BK	Biblischer Kommentar
BRL	*Biblisches Reallexikon*
BS	*Bibliotheca Sacra*

BSt	*Biblische Studien*
BT	*Bibliothèque de théologie*
BVSAW.PH	Berichte über die Verhandlungen der sächsischen Akademie der Wissenschaften zu Leipzig, philologisch-historische Klasse
BWANT	Beiträge zur Wissenschaft vom Alten und Neuen Testament
BWAT	Beiträge zur Wissenschaft vom Alten Testament
BZAW	Beihefte zur ZAW
BZ NF	*Biblische Zeitschrift,* Neue Folge
CAB	*Cahiers d'archéologie biblique*
CAT	Commentaire de l'Ancien Testament
CBC	Cambridge Bible Commentary
CBQ	*Catholic Biblical Quarterly*
cj	conjecture
CSCO	Corpus Scriptorum Christianorum Orientalium
CTh	Cahiers Theologiques
CThM	Calwer Theologischer Monographien
DB(9H)	*Dictionary of the Bible,* ed. J. Hastings
DBS	*Dictionnaire de la Bible.* Supplement
DB(V)	*Dictionnaire de la Bible.* Vigouroux
DIS	*Dictionnaire des inscriptions sémitiques de l'ouest*
DLZ	*Deutsche Literaturzeitung*
DThC	*Dictionnaire de Theologie Catholique*
EB	*Encyclopaedia Biblica*
EJ	*Encyclopaedia Judaica*
EJ(D)	*Encyclopaedica Judaica.* Berlin
EKL	*Evangelisches Kirchenlexikon*
Est Bib	*Estudios Bíblicos*
ÉtB	Études Bibliques
EThL	*Ephemerides Theologicae Lovanienses*
ÉtOr	Études Orientales
ÉTR	*Études theologiques et religieuses*
EvTh	*Evangelische Theologie*
EzAT	Erläuterungen zum Alten Testament
FRLANT	Forschungen zur Religion und Literatur des Alten und Neuen Testaments
Gk	The Septuagint
HAB	Harper's Annotated Bible
HAT	Handbuch zum Alten Testament
HBK	Herder's Bibelkommentar
HIsl	*Handwörterbuch des Islam*
HLa	*Heilig Land.* Nijmegen

HSAT(K)	Die Heilige Schrift der Alten Testaments, ed. E. Kautzsch
HThR	*Harvard Theological Review*
HTS	Hervormde Teologiese Studies
HUCA	*Hebrew Union College Annual*
IB	*Interpreter's Bible*
ICC	International Critical Commentary
IDB	*Interpreter's Dictionary of the Bible*
Interp	*Interpretation*
JbAC	*Jahrbuch für Antike und Christentum*
JBL	*Journal of Biblical Literature*
JE	*Jewish Encyclopedia*
JETS	*Journal of the Evangelical Theological Society*
JJS	*Journal of Jewish Studies*
JNES	*Journal of Near Eastern Studies*
JPOS	*Journal of the Palestine Oriental Society*
JTS	*Journal of Theological Studies*
KAI	*Kanaanäische und aramäische Inschriften*
KAT	Kommentar zum Alten Testament
Kath	*Der Katholik*
KBL	L. Köhler and W. Baumgartner, *Lexicon in Veteris Testamenti Libros*
KEH	*Kurzgefasstes exegetisches Handbuch*
KEK	Kritisch-exegetischer Kommentar über das Neue Testament
KHC	Kurzer Hand-Commentar zum Alten Testament, ed. K. Marti
KK	Kurzgefasster Kommentar zu den heiligen Schriften Alten und Neuen Testamentes
KlSchr	*Kleine Schriften zur Theologie*
KrR	*Krest' anská Revue*
KuD	*Kerygma und Dogma*
KVHS	Korte verklaring der Heilige Schrift
LBC	Laymen's Bible Commentary
NAWG	Nachrichten der Akademie der Wissenschaften in Göttingen
NThT	*Nieuw Theologisch Tijdschrift*
NTT	*Norsk Teologisk Tidsskrift*
OTL	Old Testament Library
OuTWP	*Die Ou Testamentiese Werkgemeenskap in Suid-Afrika,* Pretoria
PastB	*Pastor Bonus*
PCB	New *Peake's Commentary on the Bible,* ed. M. Black and H. H. Rowley
PEQ	*Palestine Exploration Quarterly*

PrincThR	*Princeton Theological Review*
RB	*Revue Biblique*
RBíblArg	*Revista Bíblica* (Argentina)
RE	*Realencyklopädie für protestantische Theologie und Kirche*
REcL	*Revue ecclésiastique de Liege*
RÉJ	*Revue des Études Juives*
RGG	*Religion in Geschichte und Gegenwart*
RHPhR	*Revue d'Histoire et de Philosophie Religieuse*
RLA	*Reallexikon der Assyriologie*
RQ	*Römische Quartalschrift für christliche Altertumskunde*
RSÉHA	*Revue Sémitique d'Épigraphie et d'Histoire Ancienne*
SBh	Stuttgarter Bibelhefte
SB(PC)	Sainte Bible (Pirot/Clamer)
SBi	Sources bibliques
Scrip	*Scripture*
Sem	*Semitica*
SjTh	*Scottish Journal of Theology*
SSN	Studia Semitica Neerlandica
StD	Studies and Documents
Strom	*Stromata*
TBC	Torch Bible Commentaries
TDNT	*Theological Dictionary of the New Testament* (Eng. trans. of *ThWNT*)
THAT	*Theologisches Handwörterbuch zum Alten Testament*
ThB	Theologische Bücherei
ThL	*Theologische Literaturzeitung*
ThPQ	*Theologisch-praktische Quartalschrift*
ThQ	*Theologische Quartalschrift*
ThR	*Theologische Rundschau*
ThST(B)	*Theologische Studien*, ed. Barth
ThStKr	*Theologische Studien und Kritiken*
ThWAT	*Theologische Wörterbuch zum Alten Testament*
ThWNT	*Theologische Wörterbuch zum Neuen Testament*
ThZ	*Theologische Zeitschrift*
TOTC	Tyndale Old Testament Commentaries
TRE	*Theologische Realenzyklopädie*
TUAT	*Texte aus der Umwelt des Alten Testaments*
UT	C. Gordon, *Ugaritic Textbook*
VF	*Verkündigung und Forschung*
VT	*Vetus Testamentum*
*VT*Suppl	*VT* Supplement

Abbreviations

WA	Weimarer Ausgabe of Luther's works
WAAFLNW	Wissenschaftliche Abhandlungen der Arbeitsgemeinschaft für Forschung und Lehre des Landes Nordrhein-Westfalen
WdF	Wege der Forschung
WMANT	Wissenschaftliche Monographien zum Alten und Neuen Testament
ZAW	*Zeitschrift für die alttestamentliche Wissenschaft*
ZDPV	*Zeitschrift des deutschen Palästina-Vereins*
ZKTh	*Zeitschrift für katholische Theologie*
ZLThK	*Zeitschrift für die (gesamte) lutherische Theologie und Kirche*
ZNW	*Zeitschrift für die neutestamentliche Wissenschaft*
ZRGG	*Zeitschrift für Religions- und Geistegeschichte*
ZThK	*Zeitschrift für Theologie und Kirche*

Index of Hebrew Words

Index of Hebrew Words

Index of Biblical References

Index of Biblical References

Index of Names and Subjects

Index of Names and Subjects